Do Something Else

Do Something Else

The Road Ahead for the Mainline Church

NATE PHILLIPS

CASCADE *Books* · Eugene, Oregon

DO SOMETHING ELSE
The Road Ahead for the Mainline Church

Cascade Books
An Imprint of Wipf and Stock Publishers
199 W. 8th Ave., Suite 3
Eugene, OR 97401

www.wipfandstock.com

ISBN 13: 978-1-4982-2639-4

Cataloging-in-Publication data:

Phillips, Nathaniel D.

Do something else : the road ahead for the mainline church / Nate Phillips.

xiv + 138 p.; 23 cm—Includes bibliographical references.

ISBN 13: 978-1-4982-2637-0

1. Church work. 2. Church. 3. Christian leadership. 4. Christianity—21st century. 5. Pastoral theology. 6. Discipling (Christianity). 7. Missions. I. Title.

BV600.3 P44 2016

Manufactured in the USA.

To Ari, Grace, Lily, and Max

"I don't deny that there should be priests to remind men that they will one day die. I only say it is necessary to have another kind of priests, called poets, actually to remind men that they are not dead yet."

G.K. CHESTERTON

Table of Contents

Foreword

I am old enough to remember walking into the grocery store and there being one or two, *maybe* three, real choices for any product on the shelf. And regardless of the product, be it mayonnaise, cereal, or detergent, there was always the one big brand . . . the go-to company . . . the one that more people than not, knew, understood, and trusted to bring into their homes.

Today, when I walk up and down the grocery store aisles, my senses are overwhelmed by the number of choices and variables that most products offer: where it was produced, what it is made of, how much it costs. In my grumpier, old man moments, I hanker for the good-old-days when there was one kind of peanut butter, one kind of beer, and one kind of detergent. And then I remind myself that my own grief over the loss of times gone by does not mean that, if those times were brought back today, they would be successful. Since companies have fully embraced this new reality of choice so it impacts our shopping experience in the world, it should come to no one's surprise that our social lives have been impacted as well—namely that there is no longer *one* way to be community.

This world of choice and niche culture is one that the church must grapple with in faithful ways. Rather than yearning for days gone by or believing that "if we just try harder" or "wait it out" all will return to the way it was, we must live out this opportunity to be diverse and expansive communities of faith in the world. The days of broad denominational influence have passed, and while there was good work done through that particular time of the church, now is the time to embrace, celebrate, and unleash new ways of being church.

In *Do Something Else*, Nate offers us a weaving together of his story with the stories of others, all seasoned by a genuine excitement about the church. As he does so, Nate clearly claims his own social location and context while bringing in voices that, like that supermarket, expand our

understanding of what the church is and can be beyond the days of obliga-
tory denominational loyalty. The heart of this book is that in the varied
contexts and the voices that are heard around race, style, sexuality, geogra-
phy, socioeconomics, etc., we are given a hopeful and textured view of the
church today. But unlike a shopping aisle, this is not about a product to sell
made up of different ingredients or snazzy labels, but a nuanced offering of
church that is inspiring, imaginative, and incarnational.

Do Something Else is NOT a book that intends to give a list of "how-
to-do" church tips to save any particular faith location, but one that simply
asks the question, "What if?" in order to inspire and give texture to the
idea that the church is and can be so much more than we can imagine. So
read this book, not as a command to go and do something specific, but as
a powerful encouragement to go out and be the church in ways that are
specific to the community into which it is called to serve.

Many thanks to Nate and the voiced gathered in these pages—you
have inspired our imaginations.

Peace be with you,

Bruce Reyes-Chow

\

Preface

I took on this book project in the same summer that I learned how to swim. My original goal was to do an Ironman event, which entails over two miles of swimming, over a hundred miles of biking, and a marathon (26.2 miles) run. This was a terrible goal for a variety of reasons, but mostly because, when I made the goal, I could not swim to the end of the pool and back without stopping. I tried to teach myself through online videos and an assortment of books. I forced myself to get into the pool everyday, believing that if I just kept at it then it would click. It didn't.

So I started picking the brain of every swimmer I knew. My friend Katie told me to get my chest down. Mike told me to keep my head still. Ian said to swim on my side. Every time I went to the pool, I listened to their voices in my head. Even with my head under water, I heard them cheering me on.

This is kind of what it has been like to write this book. For starters, I am not an expert. I am not an expert at church or innovation. I, like most every church person that will read this book, am doing well if I am still afloat after a lap or two around the ministry pool. The people you read about in this book are amazing, but they would probably say the same thing.

Second, this book, like all of the swimming resources I purchased, is not magical. You will not read the book and then, immediately, be able to do something you could not do before. In fact, while I concede that there are prescriptive elements in these chapters, you are about to read more of a love story than a recipe book. It is a love story to the mainline church, to Mission at the Eastward, to my hometown, and to the Spirit of God moving through it all. Forgive me if (when) I get a little bit gushy.

Finally, all of this writing comes by way of a lot of cheerleading. Everyone knows that when you take on something big, no amount of "keeping at it" can compare to the voices that manage to inspire even when you're in over your head.

My wife, Ari, walked with me through the proposal process, helped make time for me to write, and has read every word of this more than once. I love when she reads because she always tells me it's great. Even when it's not.

My brilliant friends, John Molina-Moore, Edwin Estevez, Jason Brian Santos, and Diane Janssen Hemmen are my reality check. A contrast to Ari's unconditional affirmation, these four have never heard an idea that they think is perfect. I love that about them.

Through the graciousness of all that goes with a sabbatical leave, Red Clay Creek Presbyterian Church, New Castle Presbytery, my co-pastor, Patrick Vaughn, Director of Music, Jeffrey Miller, and Office Coordinator, Julie Reeder gave me the time to sit, think, and type without worrying about my day job.

Then there are the company of ministers and church leaders featured in these pages. Many of them took a cold call from me and welcomed me into their ministries. They trusted me to write their stories and are trusting you to hear them well.

Thanks, too, to those that made introductions. I am indebted to Ian Markham, Jessicah Duckworth, Carol Howard Merritt, Bruce Reyes-Chow, Tom Dickelman, Lindsay Armstrong, Andrew Root, Andrew Tibert, Tim Rodden, and Drew Dyson for connecting me to one name or another.

I am grateful for Bruce Reyes-Chow, Matthew Bruce, and Scott Planting, who were willing to attach their words to mine. These three gentlemen are exceedingly brave and kind.

I am forever indebted to the people of Mission at the Eastward for being a lifelong "Giving Tree." This cloud of witnesses includes my mom and dad, Grammy and Grampa L, Grammy and Grammy P, Auntie, Uncles, and baby sisters who, with Scott, Karl, Jeff, Carl, Babbie, Ward, Stu, Vivian, Dolores, and Dori all raised me up to be "Wicked Good." Especially, this time, I am thankful to Joni James and Amber Sturtevant who offered their own expertise in art and editing to bring this book to life.

Finally, to my children—Grace, Lily, and Max—who inspire me to believe in so much.

Days before I finished the first draft of this book, I completed my triathlon. It was a sprint event, not an Ironman, which meant I only had to swim a third of a mile. It didn't matter how short it was; I was still terrified to get in the water. When the gun sounded and a hundred of us started swimming, I found that there was no room to do the freestyle swimming I had been training so hard to do. Everyone was pushing and tugging and flailing to move through the water. A few of the best swimmers might have been out ahead with good technique, but the rest of us were doing something else. It wasn't *graceful*, but it was *something*, and we didn't sink.

So, come on in, church, the water is fine. Come in to splash with stories of love and life. Come in to float on the waves of our tradition. Come in and get drenched in the goodness of people who pray, sing, eat, and laugh together. But come in knowing that there is something about our water, the Living Water, that has a way of plunging us under, if only just for the thrill in pulling us back up!

PART 1

Where We Are

CHAPTER 1

Good Old Stones

I spent my earliest childhood years living in a church manse. I am a pastor, so this news is probably not much of a surprise. Many of my friends from seminary grew up in church manses, just like I did, because their moms or dads were pastors.

But neither of my parents was a pastor.

My parents were both eighteen years old when I was born on September 25, 1977 in Skowhegan, Maine, or Skow-Vegas if you're a local. My father had a job milking cows at a small-town dairy farm, then he sold Electrolux vacuum cleaners, and ultimately got a job "chopping" for a logger. I can remember that he got paid $300 cash a week and we were thrilled. We thought we were rolling in it. Soon after, and much to my mother's chagrin, dad bought a Nintendo.

She worked too. She was a seamstress and sewed wedding dresses for my Aunt Caroline's sewing business. Like pastors, my parents worked hard everyday, but my dad, my mom, my two kid sisters, the occasional dog or cat, and a variety of varmints and moths lived in this church manse in West Mills, Maine, because that's all we could afford.

The local church that owned the manse only billed us $50 per month to stay there and my guess is they didn't even collect it most of the time. Perhaps they felt a bit guilty. After all, the house let in a frigid draft, but, like most Mainers, we put heavy plastic on all the windows and kept the wood stove going nine months out of the year. It didn't have hot water or a flush toilet either. Ultimately, we did get an outhouse built on to the side of the house to replace the one we had to walk out to in the backyard; a welcome respite in the throes of winter.

We also had a dug well (as opposed to a drilled well or town water) set off from the house. The well was covered by two mammoth gray stones and they doubled as my playground. I rode on them, climbed over them, and created worlds on top of them. I might've even dropped little things down in between them. In any case, these stones were a sanctuary.

Then, one day, while I was playing on the gray stones, the strangers arrived in a fancy van. My mother told me that they were "church folks," but they were strangers to me, so I half-hid behind the stones and watched. These strangers moved very quickly; they seemed worried about the time. They knocked on the door, and one of them, a woman, said something to my mother. Another adult, a man, led the others to our porch steps, and before the woman was through with my mother, they started peeling the wood off the stairs of our front porch. The loud sound of the cracking boards echoed through the village. They didn't seem angry or happy, but they were definitely in a hurry, so I stayed put behind the best stones in the world.

It wasn't long before they were replacing the old wood with fresh boards. Even though they were still in a rush, getting the new boards nailed on "just right" took them a really long time. I was patient and, thankfully, the stones were too. We just waited. What was it that made me wary of these people? Was it their van? Perhaps. After all, it was the most expensive vehicle that ever graced our driveway. Or maybe it was the way they treated my mother. Or maybe it was the way they talked with one another in half-whispers so nobody inside the house could hear. Whatever it was, I knew I didn't trust these people.

It seemed to take them forever, but eventually they huddled together next to our house and took a picture. I thought the porch looked kind of funny with all of those new boards; it looked really out of place next to our old house, but it seemed to make the fancy-van-people happy to have it done, so they left. Finally. To this day, I'm not sure if they ever noticed me sitting there.

Good old stones.

It is partly from this perspective, from behind those good old stones, that I offer the stories in this book, because living in that house taught me many important things. Not the least of which is that the church can't fix everything. Even the best efforts of the church will come up lacking. Even the most committed to helping and healing will leave some kind of hardship behind. Even the best churches, and this will surprise them and disappoint them someday, will be unable to fully repair what is broken.

But it taught me this too.

The church can do *something*.

I will never forget that old house.

It is painted red now. I think it was green then.

I wish I could say I have some great memory to share from my time spent there. If I thought long enough, I could probably come up with something. But it is the gift that the church gave to my family, having us live there and everything that went with that. Looking back on it now, I don't mind saying, it's a big part of how Jesus crept into my heart.

Which brings me to the other perspective from which these stories are told: the "church folks" that came to our little manse were from a suburban church in New Jersey or Pennsylvania. I'm not exactly sure where. Many of these kind souls made, and still make, the trek up I-95 to visit rural Maine and a cooperative parish of nine very small Presbyterian churches called "Mission at the Eastward" or MATE.

Born from a chance assignment by the Presbyterian Church's Board of Sunday School Missions in the early 1940s, MATE cannot boast about worship attendance or budget growth in any of its churches. It can and should, however, be proud of its ongoing summer camp ministry, "Sparrow's Nest" community theater program, gardening partnership with a church in South Africa, and, of course, its housing ministries. It is stunning to sit back and reflect upon the consistency and dedication that the people of MATE have had in coming alongside the poor and lonely. Of all the mission statements and church mottos I've ever seen, I've never seen one as appropriately encompassing as MATE's: "To Reach the Last Home on the Last Road."

There is so much more to tell about Mission at the Eastward, and I will tell it, but, for now, let's leave it at that.

Needless to say, the Spirit-led ingenuity that brought MATE to fruition and continues to give the small organization its only shot at continued ministry in a small-budget climate, is a declining resource in today's church. MATE has never had the option of leaning on an endowment or relying on a major donor. Most of its funding comes either from the pockets of blue-collar workers (farmers, loggers, truckers, etc.) or from denominational grants, both of which demand year-over-year accountability and concrete results. "God didn't put us here to die," said Carl Geores, a pastor and key

figure in the growth of MATE, who then offered a simple admonishment—
"so *do* things."

That is where we are. That simple admonishment is the engine that
moves every word of this book. As I finish my first decade of ordained
ministry, I am increasingly aware of the importance of Carl's voice. On a
general level, I am aware of a certain despondency in the mainline church,
a church that I love. That despondency is made manifest in our commitment to the way "we've always done it," in our theological concessions to
the more conservative branches of the church, and our nostalgia for a supposed golden age of institutionalized religion.

Further, on a personal level, I long to rediscover a real, maybe even
cosmic, purpose in my work. Did I really take those ordination vows to
referee squabbles over Styrofoam cups, worship service times, and the color
of the carpet? Did I take on seminary and the clerical robe so that I could
take out the old sound system and the grumpy antagonist? Did I master the
theological and exegetical so that I could manage the janitorial and admin-
istrivial? That is where so many of us are.

One might think that vocational rediscovery would be initiated in the
simple camaraderie of other church folks, but that is rarely the case. Too
often, instead of hope, clichés abound. Every pastor and church leader has
their favorite one to describe ministry; some say it is like "taking sand to
the beach," others prefer "rearranging deck chairs on the titanic," or, my
personal favorite, "putting lipstick on a pig." Amidst those clichés, however,
there is a desperation that resonates with mine. There has to be something
more, something with ultimate meaning, to all of this, even if we are not
sure where to find it.

So I went on a journey, for all of our sakes. It was a treasure hunt, of
sorts. Along the way, I met the most fascinating people. They have bright
faces. They are taking risks, building favor, listening well, and creating community in ways that remind me, and will remind you, of why we got into all
of this in the first place. I, for one, am re-inspired by these exemplars. As I
am, I hope you will allow me, once and for all, to echo Carl's call to all who
read these pages.

God did not put you here to die.

So do things.

What does that admonishment look like to the mainline church outside the foothills of western Maine?

What does it look like for small churches resigned to be "without a pastor," for larger churches looking to do a new thing in an unorthodox way, or for middle governing bodies who need promising examples of working models in order to take the risk on new opportunities?

What does Carl's admonishment look like for candidates of ministry who see limited options, for clergy call-seekers trying to find hope in a desolate career landscape, or for clergy leaders attempting to manage church staffs with limited resources?

With the good old stones and Mission at the Eastward in our rearview mirror, we will begin by examining how we arrived in this place. In the next two chapters we will ask, "How has ministry leadership changed over the years?" More specifically, in chapter 2, we will take on how drastically the expectations for ministry have changed. In chapter 3, we will consider how we are slowly moving toward inclusion in mainline ministry. In both chapters we will look at the lives of ordinary ministers that represent significant shifts in church leadership. Their stories remind us that *change* is part of who we are and, as such, they urge us to willfully embark on our stage, topsy-turvy as it is, of the divine and human co-adventure.

Then, as if taking a deep breath before jumping into a deep, spring-fed lake, we will allow Dr. Matthew Bruce, a church-loving theologian, to walk us through what we mean when we say "church." Matt will confront what we typically mean when we say "church," and offer us a helpful alternative. His words will establish an important starting point in pushing the mainline church toward the road ahead.

Then, in part two, we will turn to the challenges and opportunities that are before us in the present-day ministry frontier. We will consider this from the perspective of Worship (chapter 5), New Church Starts (chapter 6), Evangelism (chapter 7), Outreach (chapter 8), Church Enterprises (chapter 9), and Cooperative Parishes (chapter 10). Through it all, we will embrace the long-held posture of Mission at the Eastward and set off toward new models of sharing the gospel. Not only because we have to, but because we really want to.

As the half-fixed porch on our old manse can attest, the church cannot do everything.

But it can do *something*.

For a long time, it's done the *same thing*.

Perhaps it's time for it to do *something else*.

CHAPTER 2

Why Would Anybody Want to Do This?

It is tempting, I'm sure, to flip to a chapter of this book that addresses a current passion or conundrum. Perhaps you are interested in new expressions of church outreach or how the mainline is reclaiming a zest for evangelism. "Why," you might ask, "do I need to hear about pastors in the 1950s and 60s when I came to find a formula for starting a coffee shop ministry or launching a new worship service?" The answer to that query is as simple as another one; "Do you really have time for something else?" I somehow doubt it. Today's pastor has a complex and, periodically, irrational list of duties to sort through before given the opportunity to talk, invite, or do anything new and creative. We can press on and dismissively pretend that they are not there, as if we are naïve enough to believe that the work of contemporary pastoring is a straightforward endeavor that offers loads of flexibility to be imaginative. But, until we unpack the expectations that pastors and church leaders face already, until we investigate what they are, why they are upon us, and what we need to do to address their value, we will not have the time or energy to do something else.

And so, our story begins, not in today's most trendy church or at the desk of a great innovator, but in the 1940s when a young lumberjack sky-pilot named William Burger landed in the mountains of Western Maine to serve alongside the loggers of the thick Maine woods. Burger, a Yale Divinity graduate, began his ministry there under the Presbyterian Board of Missions. In 1947, *Time* magazine described Burger's ministry to the community in this way:

In the bunkhouse, 70 men lounged on the benches or in the double-decker bunks, reading pulp magazines by the dull oil lamps. The rafters over the hot stoves were festooned with drying socks. As soon as the poker players cleared the cards and money from the table, the minister set up his small silver cross and two candles and began to talk. . . . First, he told them the news they wanted to hear—about how the steamer, Frost, was all set to boom the pulpwood across Lake Mooselookmeguntic. . . . After a while he worked around to religion, passed out some leaflets and invited the men to look at the Bibles and paper-covered Gospels he had piled on the table. Most of his congregation were French Canadians who understood little of what Pastor Burger had said, but they were glad to find "La Sainte Bible."[1]

This assignment marked the beginning of what is now known as Mission at the Eastward. It is a year-to-year bare-bones operation kept alive by keen eyes, warm hearts, and a healthy dash of the Holy Spirit, so it is not difficult to imagine that it all began around oil lamps and campfires.

Burger's story of ministry is the sort that still attracts would-be ministers to embrace the profession for themselves. The desire to bring comfort and good news to those living in a forest of desolation, like Burger did, runs through the veins of nearly every seminarian. His story offers the seductive promise of making an impact on people who, for the time being, hear the language of Christian faith as foreign. His legacy in a community that had no ministry presence when he arrived, but boasts so much now, is one that most new pastors fantasize about.

When Conrad Richter, the son of a Lutheran minister, wrote his short novel, *A Simple, Honorable Man*, he was writing about ministry the way that Bill Burger went about it early in his career. It is the tale of a good minister, Harry Donner, who does the right thing. He tends to his family, he visits the sick, evangelizes the mines, and he goes to great lengths to extend small kindnesses in and around his small, rural congregations. He does all of the dreamy things that pastors are meant to do. Richter's narrative also focuses on the various darker shades of a pastor's life. The sacrifices that spouses and children make for the sake of the ministry emerge as a primary storyline. He skillfully illustrates the constant and creeping shadows of self-doubt, shadows known almost universally to church leaders, in a way that only a pastor's kid could. At one point Rev. Donner confesses that

1. "Religion: Preacher in the Woods," *Time* magazine.

"he couldn't think at that moment of any real good that had come out of his ministry."[2]

At least once, though, Richter lets us in on his imagined perfect posture of pastoral leadership. It comes after an emergency call to visit and baptize a dying man on the bad side of a steep mountain. His horseback journey to "the patch" draws the attention of the townsfolk and many wait outside as he performs his intended baptism, a makeshift Eucharist, and a time of intercessory prayer. Tellingly, it is a trip that enlivens Reverend Donner's passion for ministry.

> Here in the patches they had . . . neither sheep fold nor shepherd, no Sunday school or altar, no man of God moving among them to remind them of their heavenly Father who knocked unseen on the doors of their rude houses or of the Holy Spirit ready to descend with the men in the dangerous breasts and headings of the mines. . . . When he stepped outside the men were still there, flanked now by some women and children. He sensed a respect he had never felt when out with the store team. Warmly he shook hands with them all. Several asked if he would stop in at their houses to see them.[3]

Richter's work, while based loosely on his father's life, is a brilliant piece of fiction in that it has effectively captured the longstanding pastoral archetype. That is, some composite of Richter's "Simple, Honorable Man" and Bill Burger the "lumberjack sky-pilot" remain the subliminal standard for what a good pastor does from day to day.

While romantic, this yesteryear version of pastorhood is dangerously deceptive. Research from the Schaeffer Institute reports that 50 percent of ministers leave the vestments behind within their first five years.[4] It is an eye-popping statistic on its own, but it gets worse when compared to that of other community caretakers. While pastors drop like flies, their professional counterparts hang in there. Studies of resignations from the police force, for instance, show better than average turnover rates (in relation to other public service employment) and the nursing profession regularly boasts 80 percent of its licensees continuing their work in the field.[5]

---

2. Richter, *A Simple Honorable Man*, 90.
3. Ibid., 70.
4. Krejcir, "Statistics on Pastors."
5. Sherman, "The Myth that Nurses Leave Nursing."

Could it be that pastors just need to do more devotions? In other words, can't they just pray through it? Some would argue this is the case. The Schaeffer Institute tells us that only 26 percent of pastors feel they spend adequate time dedicated to personal spirituality.[6]

Or, conversely, maybe wayward church members should be blamed for the pastoral exodus. After all, 81 percent of pastors report being dissatisfied with the discipleship program in the church because only 25 percent of their members manage to participate in Bible study or adult education.[7]

Or maybe new pastors are simply being surprised by what they are expected to do. Perhaps they thought they were getting into the religious market with the Simple, Honorable Man, but, instead, found an incomparably complex system of demands on their hands. The Schaeffer Institute's data tells us that 90 percent of pastors acknowledge that ministry was completely different than what they thought it would be like before they entered it and 80 percent feel unqualified to do what they are being asked to do as a pastor.[8]

Today's would-be pastor has little idea of what she is getting into and so it is time, for her sake, to thoroughly revisit how the role of the pastor has changed since Richter's Rev. Donner pastored in the patch. Of course, his way of doing ministry is still part of the story. Pastors still do home visits and look after the sick. Many still carry prayer books and travel long distances to be with someone in need. But, over the years, additional facets were added to the pastor's professional plate and each of these facets were given varied emphasis depending on their place in the socio-ecclesial timeline. The context is always calling the church to be something new and, so, the church is always needing its pastors to restock their vocational toolbox. Of course, when the church does this, it does not always provide the formal courtesy of informing its pastors of the shift. So, before we encourage the church and its leaders to "Do Something Else" going forward, let's take a moment to really consider how the church has already changed—and be honest about how it has expected its pastors to have changed with it.

Over the last half century or so, we've seen three major shifts in the professional expectations for ministerial leaders. For the sake of organization, we will label these emerging facets *Captain*, *CEO*, and *Community Organizer*. Conveniently, these shifts emerge quite clearly in the faces of

6. Krejcir, "Statistics on Pastors."

7. Ibid.

8. Ibid.

the three primary leaders of Mission at the Eastward covering this time period. We see the first shift (Captain) in the pastoral career of Bill Burger, our former sky-pilot, the next (CEO) is furthered in the years that Carl Geores succeeded Burger as the coordinator of Mission at the Eastward, and through the ministry of Scott Planting, MATE's latest leader, we see the most recent shift emerge (Community Organizer).

BILL BURGER

Captain

In the late nineteenth century, when the term "sky-pilot" was first used as a label, it was not with an airplane in mind. In fact, the term predated what the Wright Brothers would do in Kitty Hawk in 1903. Instead, the term was born when clergyman Frank Higgins, one of the first sky-pilots, settled down in a Minnesota log yard. When a lumberjack asked him what he hoped to accomplish through his service, Higgins responded that he wanted to pilot their souls to the sky.[9] That is just one reason why the moniker fit Bill Burger, who began his ministry amongst the woodsmen as a clear-sighted captain, quite perfectly.

In the mid-1940s, however, he stepped away from the lumberjacks and marched into Starks, West Mills, and North Anson, Maine, and conducted vacation church schools. He was met with suspicion upon arrival. What was he doing there? What did he think they had to offer? Starks and West Mills were both rural communities, heavily dependent on farming, especially the growing of sweet corn for the canning factory. The population was declining. There was no local industry and times were hard as America attempted to recover from World War II. What could they possibly have to offer this driving force of a man? And yet, ultimately, by way of Burger's captaincy, Starks (1949) and West Mills (1950) were the first Presbyterian churches organized in a new era for the Presbyterian church in Maine.[10]

Bill Burger was the prototypical pastor for his time. While, at its start, his ministry looked much like that of the Simple Honorable Man, times were changing and his natural style fit well with the change. As Craig Dykstra and James Hudnut-Beumler point out of the early and middle years of the twentieth century, "members of all the mainline churches . . . could

9. Cartwright, "Lumberjack Sky Pilots."
10. Geores, *The Journey of Faith*, 1.

point with pride to the ever-increasing numbers of missionaries in the field."[11] Marching headstrong into unfamiliar territory, as Burger was prone to do, was the mode of operation for ministers of the gospel in that time and place.

Perhaps their is no greater example of Burger's captaincy than his gutsy design for Mission at the Eastwardb which was commissioned in a meeting of the General Assembly of the Presbyterian Church USA in Detroit in 1953. He galvanized key leaders, including notable members of national boards, to meet and agree on a plan that would provide funding for work in Maine to include the parish in Starks and West Mills and the developing work in the equally small towns of Leeds, Wales, and Hartford to come.[12]

Bill Burger died in Welasco, Texas, in 2006, but the work he set in motion way back in 1953 continues its salute. Carl Geores, the CEO leader that followed after him, made sure of that.

CARL GEORES

CEO

When Carl Geores arrived in central Maine in 1952, he was not dismissive of his pastoral heritage. Donner's ministerial romanticism and Burger's ecclesial captaincy gave him his vocational roots. This is part of what makes the work of today's pastor so difficult to maneuver. Every season or so, the church subjects the pastor to new expectations and little of what was old gets left behind, it just gets added on. That didn't seem to bother Carl though.

In his personal memoir, Carl shares tender, Donner-esque moments from his early monthly reports. He tells how, on a visit to a small hamlet back off from a main road, he met an "old lady who looked at me from her sick bed and said, 'I had given up hope that God would ever send anyone here. No one has ever cared.'"[13]

In another entry he remembers serving communion for the first time on October 5, 1952.

"The organist played 'Just As I Am' and people start to file down into the front seats to receive communion. I shall never forget it as long as I live.

11. Dykstra and Hudnut-Beumler, "National Structures," 318.
12. Geores, *The Journey of Faith*, 16.
13. Ibid.

Twenty-nine took communion, many for the first time. I know the reality of the living church of Christ. He was there at the communion table."[14]

Conrad Richter could not have written it any better.

Burger's influence bled into Geores's ministry, too. He stormed forward to charter three different churches in Leeds, Hartford, and Wales, Maine. And yet, Carl was his own man. It was his work with MATE that distinguished Carl Geores as a CEO-type leader. MATE might have been set into action under Burger, but it became an organization under Geores. In 1974, when Bill retired from ministry and Carl was elected coordinator for the mission, upstart projects like Camp at the Eastward and Rural Community Action Ministry began to take shape with the churches as a unified ministry.

His work echoed that of many pastors in second half of the twentieth century. It was a time when denominational hierarchies were peaking and committees and councils had their hey-day. Approval systems for everything from outreach events to Sunday school curriculums were fine-tuned in a "process of bureaucratic rationalization to bring all mission boards, publications groups, even temperance associations related to the church under central control."[15]

The emergence of this "corporate model managed to deliver an incredible array of goods and services that 'sold' in the sense that they were well received by the market."[16] As a CEO pastor and leader, Geores was especially adept at packaging these goods and services. While Burger scampered in and out of one ministry dream or another, Carl began his era under an organized set of objectives.

Notably, Geores organized the D. F. D. Russell medical center for rural families, which is still in operation. Camp at the Eastward expanded to a three-week program for local children. Finally, his most satisfying accomplishment, the Rural Community Action Ministry, took off. It housed a gardening project, a food and fuel program, a ministry for pregnant and parenting teens, and a housing ministry. By the time he wrote his memoir in 1988, eighteen work groups from all over the northeast were traveling to Maine to work on low income housing projects each summer.[17]

14. Ibid.

15. Dykstra and Hudnut-Beumler, "National structures," 316.

16. Ibid., 318.

17. Ibid., 88.

SCOTT PLANTING

Community Organizer

It is appropriate to leave off with Carl Geores by noting the RCAM housing ministry because, ultimately, a neighborhood housing project would be among Scott Planting's finest achievements. Also, like Carl before him, Scott embraced, even to the point of exhaustion, the expanding expectations handed to him by the pastors he followed.

Like Richter's fictional Rev. Donner, Scott enjoyed driving the countryside for a purposeful pastoral visit. I can recall riding the back roads with Scott during an internship while in my middler year of seminary. A man from his community, not a church member necessarily, was dying away from his home. Scott packed up his camera and drove through the woods for almost an hour to take photos of the man's land. I'm sure he treasured them in his last moments.

Like Bill Burger, Scott drove forward good, innovative ideas in places they were not initially welcomed. His dedication to building a meaningful project between Mission at the Eastward and the Macfarlan Church in the Amatola Presbytery in South Africa was initially viewed as a vanity project. Scott persevered through the criticism of helping those from "so far away" when there was so much to do so close to home. Scott knew how important it was for the people of Maine, so often the ones being helped, to experience the thrill of helping. By the way, if you ever have the occasion to drive through the Tyume Valley on the Eastern Cape (and I hope you do), look at the gardens that sit next to the houses. Most of them were not there before Scott Planting arrived.

Like Carl Geores, Scott took seriously his commitment as leader of the MATE organization. In fact, when the Alban Institute did a study on MATE as a cooperating congregation, they shared that "because Planting is such an excellent, committed, and faithful leader of MATE, one layperson said that his very competence raises questions about how MATE will change when he leaves."[18]

But it was Scott's demonstrable skills and abilities around local community organization that offered a perfect fit for the next change in season for church leadership. "In the 1960s and early 1970s, this [corporate] consensus began to crumble around issues that polarized the larger society,"

18. Waldkoenig and Avery, *Cooperating Congregations: Portraits of Mission Strategies*, 185.

and in the seventies and eighties "locally based movements rather than nationally organized and maintained programs carried the day."[19]

A prime example of Scott's ingenuity on the community level comes from his development of 82 High Street in 1988. His dedication to the people of his community sparked a community-wide movement to create a coalition "with the Community Action program in Franklin County, the Maine State Housing Authority, the Enterprise Foundation and MATE to buy a low income trailer park for rehabilitation."[20] His vision was the purchase and development of thirteen standard rental units and eighteen mobile homes with a non-profit entity of Farmington citizens who would ultimately own and manage the land as rental property.[21]

This was a project that brought immeasurable local impact, but, as almost every pastor knows, ideas for the common good always bring uncommon resistance. Scott would face opposition from town councils and grouchy neighbors. When the time came for the town to spend $25,000 on a new road for the site, Planting pled with those gathered at the town meeting, "Consider the needs of Farmington people for decent low income housing!"[22] Fortunately for the Farmington community, when it came to matters of justice, Scott was never easily deterred and 82 High Street was born and is still alive and well.

BRINGING IT HOME

Seemingly, every season in the life of the church brings a shift in what a pastor is expected to be able to do. Instead of old paradigms falling away, they just pile up on top of one another—as we see in the lives of the three leaders of Mission at the Eastward. Which begs our original question, "What can today's pastors actually be expected to do?" and, if the answer is "all of the above" (as it so often is), a second question emerges:

Why would anybody want to do this?

Weeks before I left to take on seminary and charge into the ministry for myself, another of MATE's sages offered me some wisdom. This time it was Ward Holder, a lifetime pastor and proud Presbyterian. His hair was as

---

19. Dykstra and Hudnut-Beumler, "National structures," 318.

20. Geores, *The Journey of Faith*, 58.

21. Austin, "Farmington Voters Give Ok to Road Building Funds."

22. Ibid.

white as any hair I've ever seen and his face had the weathering of a lobster-man, but he had a knowing twinkle in his eye.

"Nate, if you can do anything else," he glared and whispered, "do it."

Almost every pastor has a story like this and, like almost every pastor, I always assumed that he was guiding me to reconsider the plunge into ordained pastoral ministry. I suppose that might have been part of his purpose. Now, though, I am beginning to wonder if he meant something more. I wonder if what Ward had in mind was not a warning to avoid the ministry but an invitation to resist the paradigm of ministry that he and his colleagues had helped to create.

Reverend Holder died a few years ago, so I'll never have the chance to fully substantiate my suspicions. So, for now, I'll simply choose to believe that he wasn't, with cynicism, saying, "Do something else, outside of church ministry." Instead, he was, with hopefulness, encouraging, "Inside of church ministry, do something else."

Perhaps that means it's time to take all that we know about church leadership as *Captain*, *CEO*, and *Community Organizer* and leverage it toward an effort to find our way back to where Bill Burger's sky-piloting landed him. That is, perhaps it's time, yet again, to locate ministry around the oil lamps and campfires where the people don't yet appreciate what we have to say.

Before we set out to rediscover where the new campfires are burning today and how we can creatively engage them, we have a bit more work to do in unpacking our recent history. The last half century of ministry did not only bring change to the expectations of a pastor, it also witnessed dramatic changes in who gets to be a pastor. It is to an overview of those changes that we now turn.

CHAPTER 3

The Road to Inclusion

Every pastor in my childhood was white, male, heterosexual (so far as I knew), and from a middle-class background. They lived in normal homes with normal cars. They had families that looked almost like everyone else's. People complained about them, but it wasn't because they were different. Actually, most complaints were about their indifference.

"Patty got sick and nobody even visited her."

"The church bulletin had six mistakes in it last week."

"Can you believe how he lets Melissa push him around?"

The men serving these small churches generally took their derision like most pastors do—with a sigh. They knew that there was always a tomorrow for their ministry, there was little use in sticking up for themselves, and, for the most part, they were doing what they felt called to do.

A ride down Interstate 95, the only real road out of Maine, told a different story altogether. While the starched-white boys of Mission at the Eastward were tending faithfully to their (sometimes) crotchety flock, much of the rest of the mainline church was doing something else. Churches and leaders outside of the confines of detached hamlets like mine in Maine were brewing up complaints of epic consequence. These complaints far surpassed the triviality of local church irritations and swept into the heart of a gospel where those left out are lifted up. They were on the road to inclusion, attacking the unjust barriers that kept women, people of color, and the LGBTQ community from the privilege of serving the mainline in ordained ministry.

These efforts, while noble and essential, left the mainline with a variety of bruises. There were perceived winners and losers in each of these skirmishes for inclusion and, on every occasion in every denomination, fighting words were exchanged, documented, and remembered. Unfortunately, while some of these bruises were only internally embarrassing, others were longstanding and even schismatic.

For instance, in 1939, when the Methodist church attempted to unite several denominations, they conceded to a form of segregation by lumping all African American churches into a group called the "Central Jurisdiction." In an attempt to rectify the situation, in 1948, they legislated that "the principle of racial discrimination is in clear violation of the Christian belief in the fatherhood of God, the brotherhood of man, and the Kingdom of God. We therefore have no choice but to denote it as unchristian and to renounce it as evil. This we do without equivocation."[1] Slowly but surely, those words took the form of action. In 1956, the church began to allow black churches to opt out of the Central Jurisdiction and, in 1966, it dissolved Central forever. Still, it was not until 1973 that all southern Methodist conferences yielded and fully integrated their meetings.

In 1956, the first woman was ordained to serve as clergy in the Presbyterian Church. Margaret Towner, who served a church in Takoma Park, Maryland, went quietly about her ministry even after her historic ordination. She served several churches as pastor and was even the Vice Moderator of the denomination in 1981. But, as if catching up to the news of her ordination in 1973, socially conservative Presbyterian churches boiled over to form the "Presbyterian Church in America" after "opposition to the long-developing theological liberalism which denied the deity of Jesus Christ and the inerrancy and authority of Scripture."[2] The PCA continues to only ordain men in "obedience to the New Testament standard for those who rule the church and teach doctrine"[3] and remains the second largest Presbyterian body in the United States.

More recently, when mainline denominations opened ordination to those that identify themselves as homosexual, dissatisfied churches packed up and moved away in droves. In the Evangelical Lutheran Church, churches left to form New American Lutheran Church. Since its beginnings in 2009, the NALC has received at least 400 churches from the ELCA. The

---

1. Renfro, "The Reunification of American Methodism, 1916–1939."

2. "A Brief History of the Presbyterian Church in America," *Presbyterian Church in America*.

3. Carter, "How to Tell the Difference Between PCA and PC(USA)," *The Gospel Coalition*.

Episcopal family experienced the painful loss of 900 congregations who moved outside their umbrella to form the Anglican Church in North America because of decisions made concerning those in same-sex relationships. Finally, a similar movement took place in the Presbyterian Church where "The Evangelical Covenant Order of Presbyterians" received over 200 congregations from the PC(USA).

The journey toward inclusion has not been easy. In his book, *Prayers*, Michel Quoist writes that those that preach the gospel will "soon frighten away many of those now filling the church, and attract those now shunning it."[4] Churches, members, and leaders in the mainline are hoping for this to be true. Even beyond the conviction that we should work tirelessly for the dignity and personhood for all people, the hope remains that this work has strengthened our witness to the life and love of Jesus, that we are better for having an open table, and that our churches will be renewed by a fresh mosaic of leadership that looks very different to the one most of us remember from childhood. Included in that mosaic are the faces of Demetrio Beach, Shannon Kershner, and Broderick Greer.

DEMETRIO BEACH

Associate Pastor for Discipleship Ministries
Trinity-First United Methodist Church
El Paso, Texas

When it comes to progress, everything is relative. Demetrio Beach, a twenty-something year-old, African American leader in the United Methodist Church, has first-hand experience of that. Though the segregated Central Jurisdiction was dissolved with the denomination's merger in 1968, the ugliness of it lives on in a less visible form. Demetrio admits, "We still have racism in our system. It's difficult. We've been told to pray about it. 'Just pray about it,' they say, 'and it will get better.' That's what we live on most of the time."[5]

Landmark denominational decisions can bring light to important issues and put cracks in evil arrangements, but they don't put the devil to bed. By and large the mainline church, which includes Demetrio's Methodists, remains white at heart. The mainline is loyal, perhaps even blindly so, to the

---

4. Quoist, *Prayers*, 106.

5. Demetrio Beach, telephone interview with author, June 26, 2015.

way it has always been. This loyalty is so ingrained that it resists the consideration of even the smallest degree of inculturation; save for the occasional gospel chorus on Pentecost Sunday[6] and Good Friday,[7] the church pushes back on almost any unfamiliar enrichment of its tradition.

In his book, *God's Potters*, Jackson Carroll illustrates the resistance. He first acknowledges how many immigrants to the United States come with a Christian background. Then says, "the Christianity that these new immigrants bring with them, however, is considerably different from the European version brought by immigrants who came in large numbers in the late nineteenth and early twentieth centuries."[8] And yet, the mainline has communicated that they have no place for "Mariachi bands brought by Mexican immigrants, healing rituals of African immigrants and Native American congregations, or Buddhist traditions that are often incorporated into Chinese Christian practices."[9] It is no wonder that these populations are finding their church homes elsewhere.

As it is with immigrant populations, so it goes for just about any non-white group looking to join up with the mainline. In the case of the United Methodist Church it's regrettably clear, while power brokers patted one another on the back upon the dissolution of the Central Jurisdiction, the message from the white church communicated, "You can join us," instead of "We can join together." Which is why, for many African Americans, the Central Jurisdiction is looked back on with a degree of fondness. In fact, some who remember it sound like the starving Hebrews in the wilderness who looked to Moses and said, "If we knew it was going to be like this, we would've stayed in Egypt!"

Retired Bishop Forrest C. Stith rightly notes that, "When reunion finally became a reality in 1968, I knew the beneficiaries of this new church would not just be African Americans in the Central Jurisdiction but whites as well, for we brought with us not only a property or resource gain, but we brought a deep spirit of faithfulness and the love from one another that could not be transcended."[10] Even still, African Americans had the foresight to create a variety of black advocacy groups for fear that they would lose their position in this new, immense system. Most notably, in 1967 the Black

6. Every Time I Feel the Spirit.

7. Were You There When They Crucified My Lord?

8. Carroll, *God's Potters*, 43.

9. Ibid., 44.

10. Bloom and Gilbert, "United Methodists achieve milestones despite differences."

Methodists for Church Renewal (BMRC) initiated their ongoing work around the question, "How do we ensure that there will be a permanent place for blacks in the new United Methodist Church?"[11]

That question is still being asked. Demetrio offers, "Most folks now will still tell you that they miss the old Central Conference, or how things were. They will tell you how they really wish they had an African American bishop. You have to remember, before the merger in 1968 we had a lot of African American bishops and when we merged we lost that voice."

Demetrio's conference, Peninsula Delaware, received its first African American bishop in 2004. "For a conference that's been united for almost fifty years," he notes, "we received our first African American bishop in 2004 and we have about 280 African American churches. So you have people that will say, 'If only we could go back to the Central Conference. Our churches were vibrant and fruitful.'"

Demetrio does not count himself as one in that group. He is committed to leadership in a church that moves forward in the journey of inclusion. At only twenty years old, he was elected as a conference lay leader and served on the synod council for over seven years. At an early age, he has learned how to navigate around the inherent racism and ageism and bring a fresh perspective to social norms. For instance, Demetrio is committed to serving in white structures.

He says, "My friends laugh at me; they tell me I'm different. I chose to step into the white church. My membership is in a white church. I've only staffed at white churches. I want to show the church that it can happen, it can work, and we can cross the racial barriers. It is sort of taboo to have cross-cultural appointments, but that's not who we say we are. We say, 'Where God calls you, you will go.'"

The road to reconciliation in the Methodist church was cleared when it merged in 1968, but it is being walked by leaders like Demetrio. As hierarchies continue to wink at past grievances and point to ministry plans as if they were achievements, local leaders with a concern for the voiceless are creating real change. "There are persons who can't speak up," Demetrio says. "When people invite me to join boards, I tell them, 'I don't shut up.' They say, 'We know, that's why you're here.'" As Demetrio, and those like him, remain committed to this task, the church will be more than merged, it really will be *united*.

---

11. "Our History," *Black Methodists for Church Renewal.*

SHANNON KERSHNER

Senior Pastor at Fourth Presbyterian Church
Chicago, Illinois

Shannon Kershner's call to the imposing pulpit at Fourth Presbyterian in Chicago sent a healthy current of ecclesial electricity through the leadership paradigm of the mainline church. It was not just because she was leaving the picturesque backdrop of ministry in Black Mountain, North Carolina, for the frost of the Windy City. It was not just because she dared to preach in the shadow of longtime pastor and pulpiteer, John Buchanan, even if she was only forty-two years old. And it was not just because Fourth Presbyterian enjoyed, at 5,500 members, nearly ten times the membership of her previous call. Her call jolted the mainline because it offered tangible evidence that the church is finally making room for women in the most prestigious clergy posts.

Her position has other personnel and search committees asking, at least anecdotally, "If Shannon and Fourth Presbyterian can do it, why can't we?" The data is backing up the anecdote. Jackson Carroll suggests that "despite the real and often unjust barriers to the success of clergy women in traditions that now ordain women and continuing resistance to their orientation in other denominations, cautious optimism seems warranted."[12] In the 1990s, Barna reported that fewer than 5 percent of mainline Protestant churches were led by female ministers, by 2009 that number had risen to 10 percent[13] and, in 2014, the Parish Paper pushes that number to 20 percent.[14] It's a rapid assent sure to pick up steam with churches like Fourth leading the way.

Of course, Shannon does not want to take all the credit for that; partly because there is more work to do. Carroll's research contends, "women still face unequal access to higher-paying positions. Among mainline clergy in their second decade of ministry, 70 percent of men were serving medium or larger sized churches compared to 37 percent of women."[15] Shannon insists, "I'm not the first clergywoman to serve a large church. I'm very aware that there is a generation ahead of me that had to be on the front lines. The

12. Carroll, *God's Potters*, 71.

13. "Number of Female Senior Pastors in Protestant Churches Doubles in Past Decade," *Barna Group*.

14. Banks, "Women Take the Reins at Three Tall-steeple Mainline Churches."

15. Carroll, *God's Potters*, 71.

generation ahead of them had to be more radical. All of that allowed me to just be myself without having to focus on advocacy for my gender in ministry because they did so much of that hard work. I never want to be seen as if I've broken the stained glass ceiling."[16]

And yet, she is ready to accept the sobering sub layer of pastoral pressure, a layer not experienced by most male colleagues. "I absolutely feel like I have to be a champion. If I screw this up, it's going to be a reflection on clergywomen, not on 'Shannon.' That's always the case, isn't it? You get one dysfunctional clergywoman and people say, 'We can never have another woman pastor.'" The margin for error is always slim when it comes to church leadership, but that Shannon's margin is slim *and* for any slip to be fraught with such steep repercussions for an entire gender of people, means the mainline still has a great deal of work yet to do with regard to gender issues in the journey toward inclusion.

That work, at least in Shannon's mind, can begin by investigating the language we use for God. She laments, "There are still issues of language and images of God. People still have issues with hearing the gospel from a first soprano voice. It is still hard for some people to see me as a spiritual authority in their lives. But that is fewer and fewer."

She goes on, "We still have maleness as an idol. Our 'God language' is still part of our biggest struggle. It does have direct impact on how women and girls experience themselves in God's image and our possibilities. If you use feminine language for God in most mainline churches, people are going to be uncomfortable, but it broadens and changes our understanding of authority beyond patriarchy and hierarchy. It is more faithful."

That kind of faithfulness is sure to bear fruit. It communicates a sense of humility, welcome, and grace that seeps into the corners of hopelessness where it has long been lacking. Too many victims of too many abuses at the hands of too many abusers have shunned the church based on the patriarchy of church systems. But Shannon offers hope, "At every congregation I've ever served, I've had more women come to me and speak openly about domestic violence. Women come off the street when they see a female pastor serves. That makes the space that much safer and they don't think I'm going to give them the same thing they've received from other pastors."

Shannon grew up as a preacher's kid in Waco, Texas. One summer she went off to summer camp at Mo Ranch. It was there, at eighteen years old, that she sensed her first call to ministry. She was part of the acting team

16. Shannon Kershner, interview with author, May 12, 2015.

for the conference and she played the character of "Hope." As it turns out, twenty-five years later, she's still playing that part.

She is playing "Hope" for the many women and girls that wonder if a community of faith will call them into ministry. She is playing "Hope" for the women and men that have been pushed around by the patriarchy of the church. Finally, she is playing "Hope" for the mainline church as we try to be better sharers of the gospel. As she puts it, "I now know I don't need an invitation from someone else, God has invited me already to take my place. God is calling me into ministry as my whole self. I just feel like I'm able to be faithful." As she is free to be faithful, so are so many of the rest of us.

BRODERICK GREER

Episcopal clergyperson and prominent tweetalogian
Memphis, Tennessee

"Anglicanism is not as interested in answers," says the Reverend Broderick Greer, "as it is in questions and prayer, which is where I live at the moment, asking, 'Is God expansive enough to accommodate my questions and how do my questions lead me to prayer and transformation?'"[17] Being black and gay in religious traditions that have been, historically, either anti-black, heterosexist, or both, his has been a long and arduous journey to a tradition that offers him such a life-giving space for spiritual expression. The same can be said for many who, like Broderick, are identified as "other" by the privileged few who are convinced that the very existence of such "others" puts their own long-held authority at stake. Quite like the Samaritan beaten on the road to Jerusalem, the road to a faith home for queer people of any kind is cursed with those that wish to control, oppress, and shame.

Broderick found the Episcopal Church "by chance." Born into a black Missionary Baptist family in Texas, he landed in the Churches of Christ at the age of thirteen. It was in that tradition, so conservative that it refuses to use instruments in worship, that he first became a preacher as a high school student. The experience of preaching and teaching in a small, aging congregation awakened his awareness to his vocational calling. Even then, however, he sensed his patience waning for the conservative and exclusive theological vitriol marked by fundamentalist Protestantism.

17. Broderick Greer, interview with author, June 9, 2015.

On the other hand, even if he had been armed with all the patience in the world, Broderick's sexual orientation meant there never would be room for him in that faith community. Ostensibly set free from its shackles by way of his college responsibilities, he took time to explore other traditions. It was then that he first found a mentor and friend in a thoughtful Episcopal priest. He remembers, "I began to realize that I could give my whole life to Churches of Christ and keep my queer identity effectively hidden, which ate away at me severely. I was well-liked and cared for, but I wasn't being myself. It wasn't even a *piece* of myself, I was hiding my *self*—my whole, complex being—from the people I was pastoring, preventing me from being a fully capable minister. It was a one-way relationship. I knew who they were and was giving so much of myself to them, but that wasn't happening in turn. I was ashamed and isolated." Conversely, his Episcopal friend made room for his questions and in so doing became an accomplice in his faith formation.

Now, Broderick's voice is growing, dynamic, and free. A graduate of the prestigious Virginia Theological Seminary, ordained in the Episcopal Church, and boasting almost 10,000 followers on Twitter, he is curating a theologically rich conversation for the future of the mainline church. Behold a sampling of piercing questions and demanding truths from his twitter feed of over 71,000 tweets:

"I want to live in such a way that when I die, Westboro Baptist Church pickets my funeral."

"Being gay is a sin." #ThingsJesusNeverSaid.

"Gay people don't need 'curing.' Churches and societies undergirded by heterosexism and homophobia do though."

"There is no such thing as 'race' or 'homosexuality' in the Bible. Remember that."

Finally, he boldly offers a new way forward with Jesus at the lead. "The church," he maintains, "has to be interested in centering the people that Jesus would center. I've always drawn so much strength from Jesus telling the story of the woman who gives her last mite at the temple and Jesus said that whenever the good news is announced, this woman's story will be told. Not the stories of wealthy elite, but the impoverished and oppressed. I have to tell stories of the day laborers, the cafeteria workers, the crossing guards, and the people that are decidedly fixed at the margins of society at no choosing of their own. I have to say, 'This is where Jesus is, not at the center of power.'"

He suggests that the path for this kind of renewal begins with lament and leads to confession. The church has an obligation to bear sadness with and for the marginalized, especially since it has been active in the marginalization. He has experienced that firsthand. The church must lament first, for another's sake. Then it must confess, for its own.

Broderick envisions hope in all of this. "Mainline Protestantism holds within itself the potential to be an accomplice of liberation with traditionally dispossessed groups. We in the Mainline are beginning to look at ourselves in the face and say 'We are complicit in that we have dehumanized "the other" and sought to diminish the image of God in people who aren't like us.' Whether or not we realize it, that level of honesty is radical. In fact, it is actually an old Christian idea: That only through confession of sin can the process of healing begin."

The church is slowly discovering that there is a better way of being a community. It begins by giving privilege to the song coming from the throats of the dispossessed and dehumanized. It continues in sincere lament and confession. It goes on, not by our hard work or ingenuity, but, as Broderick puts it, "rooted in the paschal mystery, in the cruciform and risen body of Jesus, from which point we discover the meaning of our lives and realize that anything is possible."

BRINGING IT HOME

The road to inclusion in the church continues to bring institutional disruption to the mainline, but it also brings the paschal mystery into clearer view. Through inclusion, the church is better ready to offer something else, some other kind of presence and love to every kind of person on life's road, especially to the ones that have been left out or, seemingly, left behind—much like the little boy I met at a rest stop on I-95 one afternoon on my way out of Maine.

I met him while I was loitering outside the restroom. I stood there as husbands and fathers are prone to do; pacing about and looking at nothing in particular, and I turned to see him running in my direction. He looked to be about five years old, with freckled skin covering his skinny frame. His red hair was mostly covered up by a too-small baseball cap that was turned off-kilter. His eyes were pointed at me, but I'm sure he didn't see me. They were panicked eyes. He was just running—and he was crying.

"What's the matter, buddy?" I asked him.

"I can't see him, I can't see him!" he said to me, and his eyes continued to blaze around the room.

I was confused. "Tell me what's wrong," I said and crouched down to his level.

"I can't see him, I can't see him."

"Who can't you see?"

"Him. The person that takes care of me."

"Oh. Ok."

I did not know who this person was and there were quite a few people in the rest stop, so I was at a loss.

He began to cry again.

"I'll tell you what," I told him, "I'm going to wait right here with you until you see him. I'm not going to go anywhere."

That was all it took.

He took a breath.

He looked at me.

Then he looked, in a new way, around the room.

"There he is, I see him!" the boy said and, without looking back at me, ran to the one to whom he belonged.

As the church looks to "Do Something Else," we do well to look back and honor the "something else" that the generations before have been doing. As we do, we see something very important and instructive. We see that whatever the church does, whether it is the same as ever or something else altogether, it is only important as it does it hand-in-hand with those that stand alone, those that have been standing alone for too long, and as it stands with them long enough for them to see what they couldn't see before. As this new mosaic of voices emerge to lead the church, voices like Demetrio's, Shannon's, and Broderick's, the mainline will model inclusion, but not only that, it might find a new sense of importance.

CHAPTER 4

What We Mean When We Say "Church"

by Matthew Bruce

In the pages that follow, I turn you over to my trusted friend and brilliant colleague, Matthew Bruce. He takes a break from the ministry storytelling to offer us a solid academic footing from which to engage Part 2 of the book, "The Road Ahead." I dare say you will not find a more comprehensive, accessible, and succinct theological treatment of the word "church" anywhere.

What do we mean when we say "church"? If we are honest, we use this word in all sorts of ways to refer to all sorts of things. Upon investigation we can see that the way we use this word reveals a host of ideas, often intertwined, that point to problematic models of the "church."

First, we use the word church to refer to a place. Examples abound: a building set aside for worship, indicated with a steeple, or a red door, or a (not so) funny marquee. The place where we attend for worship, where our parents were married, where our children were baptized, and which, inevitably, always needs a new roof, or parking lot, or an organ. That other church where the boy scouts or AA meets. Often we use the word to refer to the congregation, with its glorious or not so glorious history, that has met at a particular street corner for 200 years. They met, first in small wooden chapel, then in a new brick building to which a new sanctuary was added, and then classrooms, and then a gym. A grander and grander building, that speaks to "God's blessing" and "God's glory." We will call this the "geographical-historical" model. What it reveals is our potential to make idols out of particular places.

With a little more sophistication, we use the word "church" to refer to the community of individuals who attend "*our* church" or "*that* church." We talk about how friendly the people at a particular church are, the political or social stances of a particular congregation, etc. We talk about the programs this church and that church has to offer. This one has a great youth program. That one has, choose your poison, beautiful traditional or dynamic contemporary worship. This one has a powerful preacher. That one an effective outreach program, soup kitchen, and so on. "I feel *spiritually* fed at this church," one person says. And another tells us about the youth group which the kids say "is so much fun, not boring like our old church." We will call this the "community of consumers" model. What it reveals is our tendency to think of church as a place that is supposed to meet our needs, an institution we go to acquire goods and services that we have determined we want or need.

And then there are the ideological models of "church." Often these come bundled with theological buzzwords. We might hear from the pulpit that the Greek word for "church" is *ek-klesia*, the community that is *called-out* from the world. We may hear that the church is the new Israel, the new community of God's chosen people set apart from the world. This group of set-apart individuals, distinct from the rest of the world, calls sinful people to repent and follow God's commands. We'll call this "the church against the world" model. What it reveals is our inclination to think that we alone possess the truth and that everyone else ought to think and do as we tell them. This model is characterized by pride and the desire for power.

It is little wonder that one of the most renowned theologians of the twentieth century, the Swiss Reformed theologian Karl Barth, increasingly chose to avoid the word "church" and opted for the word "community" to refer the fellowship established by Jesus Christ. He did so in order to put some distance between what he taught about "church" and such problematic models like those mentioned above. In what follows, my goal is to briefly sketch a concept of "church" that demonstrates the errors that lie behind these problematic models and lay the groundwork for a healthier model of what we (should) mean when we say "church."

What is common in the problematic models listed above is that, in each, the church (and its members) act for self-centered and self-serving reasons. In each, the church is an end in itself. The aim of each is the maintenance of the status quo, i.e., the needs of the already existing community and its members. Put plainly, the goal of activities of the church, the cause which its activities serve, *its self-appointed task*, is the church itself and its continuing existence. The building, a congregation's history, the programs and ministries, and the protection and ownership of its institutions (be they buildings or their take on the "gospel" or what have you), are thus instances of *propaganda*, i.e., arguments marshaled to defend and propagate the continuing existence of the church in a form that serves the self-perceived needs of a particular congregation. Such a self-serving community seeks to grow (add new members) primarily in order to maintain its own existence. New programs are proposed and put in place in order for this specific geographical-historical congregation to continue. The fear that characterizes such communities is that their particular congregation will die.

The problem is that such congregations are already dead. Why? Because the goal, the end, of the church is not the church. Rather, the end of the church is *Jesus Christ*, its crucified and resurrected Lord. The purpose of the church, all of its institutions and programs, is to bear witness to Jesus Christ in the world.

The models listed above are problematic because each is in fact an impediment to the true task of the church. Again, that task is to bear witness to Christ. The current theological buzzword for this is *mission*.[1] However, we must be careful here. Throughout church history, Christians have engaged in mission and missionary activity. The key thing to which we must give attention is the *intent* of missionary activity.

Let us consider "foreign missions" in the nineteenth and twentieth centuries. Christians from Europe and North America regularly went to non-Western countries to "spread the gospel." The intent of such missionary activities was, more often than not, undertaken not so much in order to bear witness to Jesus Christ, but rather to introduce the "church" and its social forms of control into the "new" world and its various cultures. Such missions were part of the colonialist systems that sought to subjugate the non-Western world to Western powers. It is often observed that the apex of foreign missions coincides with the growth of secularism in the West. At the same time that Christianity was being derided by the cultural elites of Europe and North America it was being pushed upon the "natives" in the colonies. At least one reason for this was that the various denominational

---

1. See Guder, "Practical Theology in the Service of the Missional Church," 15.

churches sought to stem their decline at "home" by reproducing themselves on the mission field. It was not the salvation of the "natives" that was the motivation for foreign missions so much as the continuation of the institutional church. As secularism gained strength and Westerners abandoned Christianity, church leaders sought to maintain their numbers, and thereby the church's existence, by replacing the "cultured despisers" of Christianity with the "uncultured" peoples of the colonies. This example should make it clear why such self-serving models of the church are instances of propaganda. They are of the same species as political messages that influence citizens to back a particular candidate by playing on their fears or advertisements that manipulate consumers into thinking they simply must have (and thus must purchase) a product for which they have no real need.

This strikes directly at the second model—church as a "community of consumers." The gospel of Jesus Christ is a not consumer good and neither is the church. If this is true, then the church is *not* a community comprised of individuals who come together because of a mutual interest in particular goods and services (e.g., a youth group, a support group, spiritual fulfillment, or even salvation from sins). I was tempted to write here that the church is not here to meet our religious needs. But this is not quite true. The purpose of the church is not to meet our self-determined religious needs, rather the church is the means by which God in Christ tells us what it means to be human beings and reveals to us our greatest need. Our greatest need is, of course, God, to be in community with God.

The consumer model is rooted in the principle of voluntary association. The individual determines what his/her spiritual needs are and chooses where to have these needs meet. The "church" is thus a place to go to consume spiritual goods, which—and this is the important bit—often merely replicates the greater society in which a particular congregation is located. The desires that lie behind the "community of consumers" model (mirroring most modern systems of consumer-driven economics) are 1) the desire to associate with people who share your distinctive social traits (race, class, culture, etc.) and 2) to maintain these pre-existing social distinctions within the church. The "community of consumers" model is, it should be obvious, clearly the chief model of the church in North America. Individual North American congregations are largely comprised of people from the same race, the same economic and social class, and the same culture.[2]

2. As an aside, it is worth noting that denominationalism itself supports existing social distinctions—though increasingly less so—in so far as the various denominations

The biblical witness is directly opposed to the consumer model. The teaching of the apostle Paul comes to a world divided culturally, economically, socially, and religiously (e.g., the Galatian church). The churches to which Paul writes are divided by factions and characterized by disunity, squabbling, and power struggles (e.g., Corinth). The constant theme of the Pauline epistles is to put aside all such divisions. For there can be no such divisions among those who are united by having been baptized into Christ.[3] The church is called to be a new community in which existing social distinction like race and class are set aside. The basis, the cause for unity, in the church is, according to Paul, Christ and Christ alone.

This does not mean that the church lacks boundaries that distinguish those who are inside and outside. Any community, as the anthropologists tell us, must have boundaries that define it. But the church is a new kind of community just because it exists to make meaningless boundaries created by nationality, race, and class. The marker that distinguishes someone from being inside or outside the church is his/her inclusion in Christ.

This may seem to lend support to the third model—"the church against the world." The third model is rooted in a faulty understanding of the church as *ekklesia,* "called-out" from the world. In the third model, the church is the place where religious truth is to be found. The "church" is understood to be situated over and against the world in such a manner that its responsibility, its task, is to call people out of the world and into itself. But the church is called to do no such thing. Rather, the church is called to go out into the world and bear witness to Christ. To use biblical language,

---

derive from and continue different nationalist identities. E.g., Presbyterians from Scotland; Episcopalians and Methodists from England, distinguished by their upper and working class origins respectively; and Lutherans from Germany, Norway, Sweden, and Denmark. Non-Protestant churches demonstrate similar patterns exhibiting near denominations within denominations. Consider the long history of Irish, Italian, Polish, and more recently Hispanic Catholic congregations, or the Eastern Orthodox Church in America with Albanian, Bulgarian, Belarusian, Greek, Macedonian, Romanian, Russians Serbian, Syrian, and Ukrainian congregations. Those congregations that are the most successful, though by no means perfectly, at resisting such shameful nationalist divisions and welcoming people of all nationalist backgrounds are contemporary Pentecostal congregations with origins in Africa, Asia, and South America. The fact that many such Pentecostal congregations are comprised of immigrant populations is directly tied to the fact that immigrants, especially when they are not "white" and at least middle class, are not welcomed in mainline, evangelical, Roman Catholic, and Eastern Orthodox congregations for they are seen as a burden that will impede the continuing, better yet recovery of, relevance and power of Christianity in the West.

3. See, Galatians 3; Bosch, *Transforming Mission,* 172.

the church is called to be salt and light in the world. Thus, far from ignoring or resisting culture, the church is called to engage culture and modify the form, not the content, of its message accordingly.

The church itself originated within a culture, at first mainly Jewish, but rapidly also Greco-Roman. For example, the polity (organizational structures), liturgy, architecture of places of worship, etc., of the "traditional" churches (Orthodox, Catholic, magisterial Protestant) are all modifications of Jewish, Greek, and Roman religious and social practices.[4] The

---

4. Examples are legion; two will suffice:

1) Communion/Lord's Supper: If we look at 1 Cor 11:20 ff. (see also the *Didache*, chapters 9 & 10) it is evident that the communion supper was actually a supper and people expected to eat their fill. In fact, they became disappointed when food ran short, with the result being enough degree of conflict that Paul had to intervene. In addition, there was enough wine that some were getting drunk, with the result being that there was not enough wine for others. Evidently the communion meal was a potluck in remembrance of Christ in which the congregation shared a meal together, likely in order to create unity by getting to know each other. Sometime after the advent of Constantine and the massive number of conversions to the church, the table for the supper became an "altar" and communion transformed from a common meal into to a religious ritual. No doubt, a major cause for this shift was simply pragmatic, a potluck meal for a house church is manageable, but organizing such a meal for a congregation with a thousand members—many new and economically impoverished—was an impossible task.

2) When the church was a minority group in the Roman Empire, clergy wore everyday clothes and were called "deacons," "presbyters," and "bishops." After the Christian faith became privileged in the Roman Empire, clergy began to wear luxurious vestments and to be called "priests" like their pagan counterparts. Why the change? First of all, the church increasingly did not have to worry about distinguishing themselves from the pagan religions, which quickly dwindled and were eventually made illegal. Cultural indicators of wealth and power signaled the falsehood of the pagan religions and the truth of the gospel. Second, the adoption of the title "priest" and corresponding clerical garments made it obvious to recent converts from paganism—who had received little in terms of catechesis—who the leaders were and what they did. Existing cultural knowledge about the office of priest, quickly established order in worship and other ecclesial affairs.

Both of these examples are often cited as evidence that the church after Constantine acquiesced to culture in ways that distorted the message of Jesus and his apostles. While we can undoubtedly point to examples where the replacement of older practices with these new practices distorted the gospel message (e.g., the creation of distinctions between clergy and laity and also the growing gap between rich and poor and the unethical power differentials that followed), there is little evidence that this was the intent in the mind of the leaders who initiated these changes. In fact, there seem to be pragmatic changes undertaken to meet the changing needs of the church, which found itself no longer a persecuted minority but the official religion of the Roman Empire. The lesson to be learned by contemporary church leaders is the need to continually examine the effect of new programs, new liturgies, etc. There may be unintended consequences such that additional changes need to be made.

early church adopted culture practices that would make the gospel of Jesus Christ intelligible and accessible in its various contexts. One of the most basic engagements with culture was the fact that the New Testament, written by Aramaic-speaking Jews who worshipped in Hebrew, was written and copied in Greek so that it might be intelligible and accessible to non-Jewish people. Another, and more significant, was the decision—a difficult and contentious one according to the New Testament—made very early in the church's life to set aside any requirements of kosher and circumcision for *gentile* converts (See Acts 15; Galatians). In the latter case, the very content of the gospel required the setting aside of the cultural-religious practices that the apostles had previously thought to be integral to the religious identities of Christ-followers. Likewise, the contemporary church should, indeed must, take up aspects of the culture in which various congregations are located in order to make the gospel intelligible and accessible. Examples of this abound: "Contemporary worship," when rightly done, intends to engage individuals in a culture that is so familiar with traditional Christian worship that they are largely inoculated against it, and are bored or, worse yet, unable to hear the good news. Later in this book, you will read about practitioners doing this with mastery by using food trucks, coffee culture, technology, and the like for the sake of reaching today's ears. They reveal how such culture engagement need not be acquiescence to culture that distorts the message of the gospel.

But it often is. And, when it is, this acquiescence is a distortion of the gospel, undertaken not to make the gospel intelligible and accessible, but rather more attractive, more palatable. As such it is a form of propaganda, the intent of which is to grow the church for its own sake, rather than to bear witness to Christ. The church and its leadership must always be alert and must always be evaluating whether new programs are instances of engagement for the sake of bearing witness to Christ or acquiescence for sake of their own desire for power and sustenance.

By now the problems with the first model are perhaps clear. Simply put, the church is not a building or an institution. It is a community united in Christ. But it is not simply or even primarily a community of individuals who are united by the fact that they are saved by Christ. Such an understanding of the church betrays an introverted stance that is still centered on the benefits of Christ accrued by the individual. The church is rather, in biblical language, the body of Christ. And as the body of Christ its task is to serve others. The church serves others by making Christ known.

What then should we mean when we say "church"? I'm going to answer this question by recovering the good that is obscured in the problematic models above.

1. *The church is the body of Christ.* If Christianity was simply a set of religious doctrines or experiences, a series of spiritual practices that need to be put into action, there would be no need for a community. But Christianity is not simply a set of teachings and practices. Christianity is faith, trust, in the person and work of the incarnate Son of God. Central to Christian faith is the confession that God became a human being and dwelt among us. As such, he has a physical body which occupies space. Jesus does not merely teach, he offers himself, his very body, to and for his followers. In order to bear witness to Christ, there must be a continuing physical manifestation of Christ's body. This is the church. For Jesus' mission to continue in the period after his ascension and before his return, he must have a community of followers who can be bodily present to others in the world. In more theological language, Christ must have an ongoing *visible body* in the world, the church is this *visible* presence. The church makes Christ known by preaching, teaching, celebrating the sacraments, serving the poor, widows, and orphans, and providing fellowship (among other things!). All of these things are equally forms of proclaiming Christ. Thus, while a designated building for churchly activities is not absolutely necessary (and is perhaps less and less so in contemporary North American culture) it is necessary for the congregation to be visible, to come together in a physical space for proclamation and worship. There must be a place to invite people to come and hear the gospel and to fellowship with each other. Thus, a church building is not a problem in and of itself. But the building and its history can become an idol when they become more important than Jesus Christ.[5]

2. *The church is a missional community.* It is not a community of consumers. But rather a *sent* community, a *giving* community. The earliest Christians obeyed the command Jesus gave them as he ascended into heaven—"you will be my witnesses in Jerusalem, in all Judea and Samaria, and to the ends of the Earth" (Acts 1:8). The aim of the New Testament writers, the purpose for which they wrote their gospels and

---

5. Perhaps the best reflection on this theme (the church as the body of Christ) in recent theology is that found in Bonhoeffer, *Discipleship*, 213–24 (chapter 10: "The Body of Christ").

letters, was to form and train up communities that would bear witness
to Christ in every corner of the globe. The message that filled them
and exploded out from them was that God has chosen all people for
salvation in Jesus Christ and, as such, all people are called to respond
in obedience, empowered by the Holy Spirit, to receive the new life
God desires for all. Justification is the overcoming of our "pride and
fall" into sin by means of Jesus' death and resurrection. Sanctification
is the overcoming of our "sloth and misery" so that we might respond
in obedience to the call to discipleship. These two classical poles of
Christ's work of redemption can be distinguished, but they are not
separate works, they are intimately connected. Christ's work justifies
us, i.e. makes us right with God, and it sanctifies us, make us holy
and fit for fellowship with God. But then what? The mistake found
in many understandings of the church is that they simply stop here.
Church members reap the benefits of Christ's work, justification and
sanctification, but for what purpose? Genesis tells us that Adam, even
before the fall, was charged by God with a vocation (he had work to
do!): "The Lord God took the man and put him in the garden of Eden
to till it and keep it" (2:15). Likewise, those human beings who are
in Christ, who are justified and sanctified, are given a vocation. That
vocation is to bear witness to the good news that the grace of Jesus
Christ is for all people everywhere. The task of the church, the vocation of all its members working together, is not to simply kick back
and enjoy the benefits of the gospel, to relax now that their religious
needs are met; rather, it is work for the sake of Jesus Christ, to be visible witnesses of Christ in the world.[6]

3. *The church is for the sake of the world.* The church is not a self-sufficient,
    independent community. Rather, like Israel in the Old Testament, the
    church is a poor, weak, often oppressed (historically, and still today in
    many parts of the non-Westernized world) community that can only
    point beyond itself to Christ. Thus, the church is not able to be in con-
    trol of its numbers, its membership—if it could, then it would be able
    to refine its message to make it more congenial to culture, to make it
    a more natural fit for its particular geographic community. But this
    would be denial of the gospel and thus of the church's life in Christ.

6. This tripartite schema of Justification–Sanctification–Vocation is the subject of
much of Karl Barth's *Church Dogmatics* Vol. 4: *The Doctrine of Reconciliation* (all 2,561
pages!)

Such an institution would not be the church of Christ but simply one more social organization—a mere voluntary society.

But the church does not have to worry about itself. The church can have absolute confidence that its Lord will take care of and protect it, much like a child who has utter confidence in the benevolent care and protection of her parent. In this freedom, the freedom of not having to worry about its continuing existence, with no fear of death, no urgent need of self-preservation, the church can get on with its task of proclaiming Christ. The church can do this because what it knows, and this is all that really sets it apart from the world, is that the entire world, each and every human being, is the object of God's eternal love. The church is simply that community of people who knows this and is charged by God with telling everyone else. This is truly a cause for the greatest joy!

PART 2

The Road Ahead

CHAPTER 5

Nodding Heads

Worship

A colleague in a nearby church ran into a personal emergency and was desperate to have someone cover her Sunday service. Their worship time allowed me to swing into worship with my congregation for the first part of our morning together and then scoot to their church. My co-pastor was scheduled to preach and I felt relatively confident that our 291-year-old church could live without Nate Phillips for half a service. I was correct.

It was a thirty-minute drive through the country and I was happy for that. Green stalks of grass and the whisper of tree leaves beckoned me out of the suburbs and toward the worship service. What a welcome! I walked into the pretty little church building fifteen minutes before the service was supposed to begin and there were six or seven worshippers there already. I slipped passed them toward the front of the church and set up my manuscript and bulletin. I slid the lapel mic onto my tie, straightened my jacket, and checked in with the organist.

I know that it is not the case for everyone but, for better or worse, it is my custom to say hello to folks before the worship service. I looked at the time and saw that I still had a few minutes, so I sauntered toward the back pews where five of the seven early-comers, all older women, were sitting. "Of course," I presumed, "they would be overjoyed to chit-chat with this bright, young, handsome-enough pastor that was sacrificing his time and expertise to bring the message of the gospel to their barren chapel."

It turns out they weren't much for small talk. Before I could even get to the middle of the aisle one of them snapped at me, "Where is our pastor?!"

41

Her eyes bore down into me. Right down past my skin and my fragile feelings and directly into my soul. I froze for a moment, stunned that they were not immediate captives to my charm, but quickly pulled myself together.

See, she might have fooled another pastor, but my church in West Mills, Maine, prepared me for this moment. I remember parishioners like her. I'm related to parishioners like her. Most of my family could be awarded an honorary PhD in dressing down the latest short-lived pastor. Which is why I just knew that underneath the sharp tongue and brutal stare was a woman who loves her church. I just knew it.

She loves her church and is disappointed every week because she comes and is joined by so few others. She knows she'll need to put together another fundraiser to keep the electricity on and she is worried that the unforeseen absence of her pastor is just another blow to getting things going.

She knows that someday soon she is going to have the chore of asking people to come back to church and stave off the suggestion that maybe it should finally close its doors. She will salve this pain like she always does, by joining with a few other obdurate members to remember and lament for the days when someone else was the pastor. They won't be able to identify why it was better, but they know that "back then" the church was something that they fear it will never be again.

If only some new people would join. Some young families, maybe. Wouldn't that be wonderful? Can you imagine if a few children came so the Sunday school could get going again? It would only take a handful. Or maybe we could get a college student that knows how to update the website or someone with a younger back that could help move the tables around for the fall festival. Everyone is getting older and the work is falling on fewer and fewer people to do the things we have always done.

She would support almost anything to make any one of those dreams come true. She would make phone calls and personal invitations. She would give a little more of her weekly money to hire a youth leader or a musician. She would do almost anything. As long as they don't change the worship service. Anything but that. This is how her mother worshiped and her mother before that. She has a long list of reasons why changing the music, order, or tone is irresponsible and shortsighted. She keeps the list in her purse. Every now and again, terror creeps in, "What if doing something else in worship is unavoidable?" She shudders at the thought.

It is difficult for her, just as it is for mainline churches and leaders confused by the attraction that so many have for a worship style that shimmers with hearty clapping, dimmed lights, electronic sounds, and pulpit-less preaching. Is it time for the mainline church to admit that it is overly-dedicated to a worship format from the 1950s? Worship leaders Nanette Sawyer, Patrick Vaughn, and Oran Warder offer a variety of answers to this question, taken together, they suggest a way forward with worship in the mainline.

NANETTE SAWYER

Grace Commons
Chicago, Illinois

Ancient Practice-Based Worship

In an interview with PBS, evangelical leader Richard Cizik bragged of how trusted church historian Martin Marty conceded in 2003, "You, the evangelicals, have won." Cizik surmised, "Well, what's he acknowledging? He's simply acknowledging that evangelicals are now the center of gravity for American Protestantism."[7] Without doubt, the mainline must acknowledge their shortcomings, especially, as Marty puts it, "trouble holding their younger generation."[8] However, amidst all the crowing that hardline conservative churches do concerning their health versus that of the mainline, they are quick to forget how many stories of disengagement they trigger. Include Nanette Sawyer in that camp.

Nanette grew up in a rural Baptist church and remembers the day that she turned away from Christianity. Her minister was visiting her at home and carried with him that version of the faith that compelled him to be her messiah, to save her sinful soul from terrors of hell. She recalls, "When I told the minister that I didn't believe these things, he left my house. And from that day on for about fifteen years I believed that I was not a Christian. I was not an atheist. I believed in God, although I didn't know how to think about God or talk about God."[9]

Her journey toward church leadership in the mainline came by way of meditation groups and a meditation master that led her into a period of healing. She went on to invest in comparative religion studies at Harvard Divinity, which led to a healthy engagement with the mystical elements of Christianity. Finally, in a cosmic response to the experience in her home those many years ago, she found herself at a communion service at a church

---

7. "Interview with Richard Cizik," *PBS Frontline: The Jesus Factor.*

8. Tippett, "Transcript for Martin Marty—America's Changing Religious Landscape."

9. Nanette Sawyer, interview with author, July 7, 2015.

in south Boston, where, she says, "something cracked open in me that night and I thought there might be room for me in the Christian church. I thought Jesus might actually be a loving figure and that the God of Jesus might just welcome me instead of condemning me. Honestly, I had never felt that before." From there, Nanette took up a call to return that favor to others shadowed by the same shaming experience of some segments of evangelical Christianity.

Today Nanette serves as pastor of Grace Commons in the Presbytery of Chicago. Her ministry is footed in, as she describes, "solid contemporary theology, rooted in history, and expressed in a non-jargony way. It is grounded in love, liberation, justice, and transformation." This philosophy of ministry translates to a different kind of church, with an innovative expression of worship she calls "Rotational Liturgy." The community meets on Sunday afternoons and welcomes a different practice each week, she explains "on the first Sunday we have a dinner and discussion called, Holy Conversation. On the second Sunday, we have Taizé Vespers, the third Sunday is Sacred Meal, and the fourth is Poetry Vespers."

Each week Grace Commons meets for worship, its participants are invited into an open forum of faith that taps into they mystical side of the Christian tradition. At Holy Conversation, Nanette offers a topic and a brief message and asks for responses through small group conversation or newsprint. At Taizé Vespers, worshipers sit in a small circle to pray the ecumenical chant-prayers born from the intentional community in Taizé, France. The Sacred Meal, inspired by Dinner Church at St. Lydia's in New York, frames a common supper with holy practice. Finally, at Poetry Vespers, various musicians and artists are invited to lead through their sharing of original compositions.

This practice-based model, while uncomfortable to some, is more than trend, but part of the natural arc in religious expression. According to Diana Butler Bass, "The first Christians believed that Jesus would restore the kingdom, medieval Christians believed that the church was the kingdom, reformed Christians believed that true Christians embodied the kingdom in word and sacrament; and modern Christians believed that they could create the kingdom through their work. But there has also been another story about the reign of God, the notion that God's people anticipate and participate in the kingdom through spiritual practices."[10]

Grace Commons is a startup ministry and one not easily replicated "one-for-one" in an existing mainline congregation. Most churches, even

10. Butler-Bass, *Christianity After Religion*, 158–59.

ones that are looking to find something new, have trouble conceiving of such a mobile model of worship. That said, Nanette insists, "We haven't figured out how to keep people engaged in a post-Christendom era. With so much transience and movement, a building or one stable location or style doesn't seem feasible in a society that is so fluid itself. We have to be able to change what we are doing based on the new information and the new participants that we are getting all the time."

That sentiment of fluidity has become a stark reality for Grace Commons. She explains, "At our strongest point we were in the art gallery and had about fifty core participants with twenty-five to thirty at the gathering each Sunday. Unfortunately, the market crashed, the building was sold out from under the neighborhood arts council, and we became itinerant." As she interprets her ministry's itinerancy and sets it alongside the nomadic experience of the people in her community, Nanette is further dedicated to wrestle with the rigidity of the mainline church. Like a pastor who attempts to break down the silo mentality of committees in a particular church, she is attempting to break down the silo mentality between churches. Her vision is for Grace to be "a true 'Commons' where members and alumni of various churches come together for creative and experimental spiritual practices at various times throughout the year."

With Nanette as a guide, perhaps the question for the church is not "How do we change or innovate our worship?" especially not "How do we shift to a flashy, contemporary style of music?" but not even, "How do we get buy-in from our members to incorporate ancient practice into our Sunday morning?" Perhaps we should, instead, be asking, "How do we join with other itinerant believers in creating altogether new worship experiences for us to be all together?"

PATRICK VAUGHN

Red Clay Creek Presbyterian Church
Wilmington, Delaware

Livestreaming

On the day Patrick Vaughn's church celebrated his twenty-fifth year of ordination, they gave him a gift. It wasn't a watch, a plaque, or a gift certificate, but a worship innovation he had been dreaming about for a long time. They

installed everything they needed to offer a Livestream of their Sunday service. Patrick reflects on the gift, "When I got here I realized that parking
and seating was limited for our primary service. I knew that many churches
were utilizing a Livestream service to set up satellite locations. I thought we
could create new worshiping communities in nearby towns and even in my
hometown."[11]

Patrick's little dream was first born when he visited a large multi-site
campus in southern California. The enormous non-denominational church
organism operated a number of venues and offered different music and
worship orders at each one. Each service shared the same sermon, preached
by the same dynamic pastor, but only one or two locations saw him "in
person," the other locations piped him in via streaming. With healthy attendance sheets and burgeoning giving records to prove its validity, it is
appropriate that Patrick, and mainline pastors like him, toy with the idea of
replicating the model in the mainline.

When he set out to actually implement his gift, he worried that it
would stall at the mercy of his minimal technical expertise. He confessed,
"I'm trying to think of a good metaphor to use when it comes to technology
and 'Mr. Potato-Head' comes to mind. I don't know much about technology." To his relief, it was much easier than he imagined. "All it took was a
modest camera, an attachment to hook it up to the internet, and a laptop.
The financial expenses are very low. Once set up, it is very easy to use. You
touch a button and it turns on, you touch a button to turn it off. We pay
about $600 a year for the hosting service. It is so simple that we have a
teenager that runs the worship slides on Sunday morning and he can do
the Livestream too."

That said, Red Clay has offered a Livestream of their service for several
years and still they do not have an official satellite, as Patrick first hoped. So
why do they keep doing it? He shares, "What we found out was that people
here are using it to a surprising degree. Particularly elderly people, people
who are sick, and can't get out of there homes. 'It feels like I'm right there,'
that's what we're hearing from people." He continues by pointing out how
many people with depression and social phobias are unable to leave their
homes but yearn for a connection with a faith community. Instead of turning to the televangelist, they can now turn to a local pastor who might be
willing to stop by for a cup of coffee or share a phone conversation. What

---

11. Patrick Vaughn, interview with author, June 4, 2015.

Patrick originally thought would be a beacon to signal a church empire, turned into a small torch bringing light to people in the nooks and crannies.

In her book, *Reframing Hope*, Carol Howard Merritt discusses the potential for "new media technologies to shape the way we tell the old, old story."[12] Like most ministers, she was taught to spend as much time as possible on pastoral visitation in people's homes. But, more and more, that type of pastoral care is becoming extinct. People are not at home they way they used to be and, when they are, they put a premium on privacy and personal space. Carol writes, "pastors, churches, and religious organizations do not get as much face time with the people among whom we minister. We have fewer sacred moments in the living room and our pastoral visits have been cut short."[13] The Livestream offers a middle way.

Steph grew up at Red Clay and is a young mother of two small and rambunctious boys. Now she lives twenty-five minutes from the church but, until recently, she still tried to make it to worship as much as possible. Then, last year, her mother was diagnosed with brain cancer and found it difficult to come to the sanctuary on Sunday mornings. These days Steph loads her kids in the car and sits with her mother in front of their large screen computer.

Anne's husband was in the final stages of dementia when her friends created "pajama church." She was committed to staying by his side so a handful of people took turns joining her at her home in their pajamas on Sunday mornings. They tuned in to the service, supported Anne in her exhaustion, prayed, and even shared communion together.

Jo is over ninety years old and faced issues with her back as a result of her leukemia treatment. As a result, she spent three months in a rehabilitation center. She always attended church on Sunday, so the isolation of the rehab center threatened to be particularly jarring on Sunday mornings. With Livestream as a Red Clay ministry, Jo was able to set up her personal tablet and told Patrick, "It was just like being there." As a result of that experience, Jo contributed funds for another church to replicate the ministry.

When Patrick first launched the worship Livestream, he encountered a small degree of resistance. Some argued that "people don't want to watch church on a little screen"' but now he realizes that, "Some people don't have any other choice. They are home with a sick kid, they are on vacation, they are on a business trip. Some people can't do this on Sunday mornings

12. Howard-Merritt, *Reframing Hope*, 78.

13. Ibid., 51.

and we've been forcing them to, almost shaming them if they don't." Now though, even if they don't have a multi-site megachurch, Red Clay Creek Presbyterian can be proud of how a little screen is making meaningful spiritual and communal connections.

ORAN WARDER

St. Paul's Episcopal Church
Alexandria, Virginia

Alternative Service

In the first decade of this century, mainline Protestant churches looked at what their evangelical counterparts were doing in worship and began to appropriate it. Over that ten-year span, for instance, the number of mainline churches using guitars and drums in worship doubled.[14] Many that did saw spiritual and numerical dividends. For instance, the study done by Faith Communities Today shows that only 17.4 percent of churches "standing pat" with their worship reported high spiritual vitality as opposed to 46.7 percent of those that were innovative and contemporary. In addition, over 60 percent of all the churches that boasted innovative and contemporary worship experienced a rapid increase in membership and attendance.[15]

The trouble for mainline Protestant churches grappling with these facts is that of maintaining their traditional identity. Many current mainline worshipers bristle at the thought of adding a screen, including a guitar, or losing the organ. For this reason, congregations with an eye for growth are looking to begin new services rather than change old ones. Oran Warder, rector at St. Paul's Episcopal in Alexandria, VA suggests that this allows "churchgoers to church shop within their own parish."[16]

St. Paul's is a large and vibrant Episcopal congregation with five worship services every weekend. Up until recently, three traditional services were offered Sunday morning with one contemplative service on Sunday evening. When "Faith@Five," the Saturday 5 p.m. service, was initiated in 2012, Oran was hesitant. "I was prepared not to like it, quite frankly." He

---

14. From 12.6 percent to 25.2 percent.

15. Roozer, "A Decade of Change in American Congregations 2000–2010."

16. Oran Warder, interview with author, May 12, 2015.

said, "I was prepared to grit my teeth and hold my nose and do it for the good of the church and because I love Jesus. But I really do love it."

The key for this service in becoming "lovable" was their starting point. Instead of predetermining what kind of music the service would have, how a screen could be added, or how the bulletin might be formatted; they invested in an internal inventory. For Oran, it was important that the new service be congruent with St. Paul's identity. "We were intentional," he says, "about really wanting to provide the breadth of Anglican experience. This wasn't about being something we're not. We are mainline. We are not going to be the place that turns into the mass crowds with hands in the air. But within our identity, we have all of these options. Why not try?" Then he advises, "The answers are within, not without. Try your best to bring the best out. Don't be boring. Let some air in. Find your vibrancy."

With that as their foundation, Oran went about building his leadership team. Settled in next to Virginia Theological Seminary, St. Paul's has advantages that other churches can only dream about. He was fortunate to have many clergy colleagues, including VTS Dean and President Ian Markham, on his team. Even still, it was his willingness to be actively engaged in developing the service that gave it real traction. While many pastors in senior leadership positions shrug off risky, innovative projects to subordinate staff, Oran knew that this project would require his relational capital.

He explains, "I contacted fifty to sixty families in the parish and asked them to make this their service for six months. I really intentionally looked for families on the edge. Folks I didn't see quite as much. Now some of them are there every weekend. I knew that if people were going to say 'yes,' I had to do it. I knew if it was going to have legs I was going to have to be involved in it."

Only then did the service itself really begin to take shape. It is set in the parish hall rather than the sanctuary, which allows for it to feel full. The preaching is excellent and mirrors the morning service, with a few tweaks to fully utilize visuals made possible by a projector and screen. Finally, of course, the music is different. Oran describes, "We have a great jazz musician that plays classic hymns with new arrangements and brings new words to familiar tunes. He has also taught us global music. It fits; it is comfortable."

Three years into the experiment, the "Faith@Five" service is finding a rhythm in the life of the congregation. Traditional churchgoers are visiting the service and giving Oran positive reviews. The leadership is beginning to see increased giving from its attendees. Most importantly, new attendees are filing in off the street. Oran admits, "On Saturday nights I'm very intentional at the end to say, 'I'm glad you've come. I hope you'll invite people. Let's share the experience.' It's the only service I say that in, because of the setting."

It is the kind of invitation that people are more and more interested in. In her sweeping research on the direction of today's church, Diana Butler Bass suggests that the church should move out of the "cerebral-believing" business and into the "participative-beloving" one. She points to the ancient church as a starting point. "The most ancient prayers of the Christian faith have nothing to do with getting ideas right. Instead, they reorder the heart, they direct it anew. Vital faith begins with desire and disposition, not a doctrine test."[17] Today's attendee is less interested in belonging to a church than belonging to the romance of God's love. They are desperate for more than poetic sermons that nod their individual heads—they want services that shape them in some way, to shape their community to do something. "People no longer join; instead, they join in. And when we join in, our hearts lead the way."[18]

Most traditional church worship services can feel very closed to a non-churchgoer. They leave little room for a foreigner to join in. The rituals and structures feel like they are for someone else, someone who grew up with them. Most churches simply accept that as reality and go about their business, catering to the consumer needs of their current members, long content to nod their heads. Some churches, growing churches, don't do that. They insist on agitating their own norms or, as Oran says, "letting some air in." Because of this, Oran and his congregation at St. Paul's have a new service and, consequently, an increasingly invitational posture.

BRINGING IT HOME

I suppose I could've packed it in when I met that woman in the back of that church. She didn't like me, at least that's what I figured. Because—can't we all agree—when someone is upset, it must always be about us.

But I just smiled at her and prepared to lead the worship service.

17. Butler-Bass, *Christianity After Religion*, 206.

18. Ibid., 205.

I preached a sermon about Samson. My exegesis was downright exceptional and my language was poetic; a preaching professor might have been impressed, but she didn't care. I am accustomed to watching heads nod as I preach,[19] but she looked out the window most of the time and, when she wasn't, she looked at the bulletin in her hands as if reading the week's announcements for the third time was more compelling than what I had to say. She never looked at me. I know this because when there are that few people in a church service, it is easy to keep track.

Toward the end of the sermon, I slipped in a connection that hopped from Samson to Jesus to us. It was a hermeneutical leap of epic, even irresponsible, proportions, but, for the first time, her chin turned toward me. It was slow the way she looked at me, as if she didn't really want to do it. But then, that woman, that crotchety woman, she smiled at me.

She tilted her head and smiled this little half smile.

And with that small movement I heard her saying, "Jesus. Oh I know him. You know him too? Why didn't you say so sooner? I've been waiting to hear about him."

Her church is struggling. It well may be that she will soon lose "church" the way she remembers it. Ancient practice is filling a void. Technology is being leveraged. Sunday morning is no longer just Sunday morning, but Sunday evening or some other time. And yet, there is a part of me that wonders if all of that will be quite alright, as long as the old, old story still gets told. As the church continues to rediscover what it means to lead worship, it might do well to trust its flock to endure "something else" as long as it remains dependable in reminding them of Jesus and his love. If it does, it might find that its worship does more than get heads nodding, but faces tilting, half-smiles forming, and whole communities taking on a new shape.

19. As if a nodding head is the primary goal of preaching and worship.

CHAPTER 6

The Widow's Library

Starting New Churches

It is among my first days here as a pastor and I am obnoxiously fresh from the protective walls of the seminary. I know almost no one in the community but receive an invitation from a woman, a widow, who lives in the retirement community, to come to her home. Hers is a request to come and visit, but more, she hopes that I will pick through her library. Her husband has only recently died and he was a pastor. There are, she suggests, some books I might be interested in and I am welcome to take whatever I like.

Confused by the layout of the retirement community, I tentatively pull up next to a small white house with wooden shutters. She opens the door before I can knock and she invites me in. It isn't easy, our conversation. I am young. I am just beginning. I am new. One day, perhaps, her husband was like me, but now he is gone. She shows me the shelves. She must be thinking about how he touched these books. How he carried them. How he wrote from them. She acts as if she doesn't need them anymore. She acts as if she doesn't want them. But how can that be?

I feel like I am invading her privacy. I am a voyeur in her library. I am looking and taking, but part of me feels like I shouldn't be. I feel like I am entering an intimate part of her world, and so I do my best to treat it as such. I flip through the pages of the books. I don't know all of the titles: some are old and, in my mind, outdated. Some are classics that I already own. Others seem interesting and I set them off to the side. Part of me wonders if I should take books that I don't even want, just to make her feel like I value them in the same way that he did—in the same way that she does. I settle on a small box of books. Later I will empty the contents of the box to various shelves in my office.

And there they sit, even today, and there they will sit for the foreseeable future, if nothing else, as a homage to her generosity and love. There is a regret in me that they don't do more than sit. I regret that the covers don't crack, that the pages don't dance in my fingers.

I fear that this is the experience of so many of today's pastors and church leaders. With almost every turn comes an expectation that the old will be useful, and perhaps even necessary, for the new. Interestingly, even as they are surrounded by the well-tended artifacts of yesterday's church, there is rarely a desire among mainline pastors and leaders to dismiss them, nor is there a rampant perception of being trapped by them. Instead, mainline pastors tend to have a healthy respect and appreciation for what has been "on the shelf," even if, like with me and the widow's books, they are not quite sure how to make use of it.

Those that serve churches with hundreds of years of history are especially prone to the imposition of yesterday. Most of these churches boast a vocal minority of churchgoers who deem it their divinely appointed responsibility to stand guard for how songs are supposed to be sung (with the organ), what makes a good sermon (three points and a poem), which families deserve special attention (the longstanding ones), and where and when pastors are supposed to stop by (omnisciently). It is an artful leader that can negotiate the expectations that come from the dusty shelf of a historical congregation, but there are many who manage all of it with great skill.

Even more artful, though, are the ones that are starting from scratch. As they "Do Something Else," these leaders are not beholden to tradition, but many are finding ways to incorporate the widow's best gifts to the great blessing of their blossoming congregations. Instead of dismissing, or even just respecting, yesterday's music, worship patterns, sensitivity to the pastoral, and commitment to service and education, the best initiators of new worshipping communities are baptizing what is old for a new season of use.

CORY MARQUEZ

New Abbey
Pasadena, California

Cory Marquez is not your typical mainline church leader. His dad was not a Lutheran minister. He did not grow up going to Episcopal summer camp.

Instead, Cory's ministry background is in the evangelical church and, quite uniquely, he is exchanging that membership card for one in the Presbyterian Church (USA). "There are a lot of experimental, innovative fresh ideas in this Presbytery," he said, "and a lot of people with these ideas are finding themselves in leadership roles. They are saying, 'Let's reinvest our money into new experimental initiatives.' They have embraced their death well and so they are experiencing a resurrection."[1]

Of course, there is more to it than that. Upon graduating from Azusa Pacific, a well-known, west-coast evangelical university, Cory began to serve in a ministerial role at one of the many large, non-denominational churches in the area. It was a growing church, but it was growing like big box stores grow, by eating up the smaller establishments and vulturing their consumers. Part of his disenchantment with the evangelical church was its idolatry to a numbers-driven model for success. He remembers his work with young adults where "it didn't matter what we did, there weren't enough lasers, fog machines, and Katy Perry songs to keep them interested."

This frustration led him to seek out voices that offered relief and it was in that quest that he met another pastor who had left the megachurch system. This man had found a great deal of numerical success in his previous work, but, as Cory relates, "he was someone that instilled in me, without intentionally doing it, there are better questions to be asked out there than, 'How are we continually appeasing shareholders that want a better show?'" It was as he explored these new questions that New Abbey was born in Pasadena.

From the beginning, Cory was committed to keeping New Abbey from parroting the pursuits of the churches around him. To do this meant keeping things simple and non-commercial, yielding to the work of the Spirit, and putting his career at risk. Some of this comes naturally to Cory, who suggests, "my greatest strength and greatest weaknesses is that I have no trouble jumping off a cliff."

That cliff looked like a small group of ten people that met regularly in his apartment to explore the vision for New Abbey. They prayed, studied, and ate together. They asked questions of one another concerning poverty and race relations in their city. Mostly though, they listened. They began as a community primarily dedicated to hearing the voices of their neighborhood without the assumption that, because they were to be a church, they clandestinely knew what the context needed.

---

1. Cory Marquez, interview with author, June 29, 2015.

This time of listening led them to establish a worshiping community dedicated to being faithful in the public sphere. To that end, they gather for worship in a public space, a coffee roaster warehouse. They commit to giving away half of their money to the public, mostly to non-profits, other churches, and people that need help paying the bills. "We are a horrible business model," Cory supposes, "but a really fascinating kingdom model."

With its commitment to a ministry of public presence, it makes sense for New Abbey to rely heavily on word of mouth, instead of church growth game planning, to gain momentum as part of the fabric of the neighborhood. "Very early on I realized that I was super uncomfortable with all of the missional language and growth theory going around my head because I realized that people don't want to be a strategy." This means that Cory doesn't retreat to an office headquarters every weekday morning but, rather, back to the coffee shop where the community meets for weekly worship. He is glad to report that the regulars jokingly refer to him as their pastor and that people outside of the church are starting to see New Abbey as an outlet for engaging significant issues in the city. Most meaningful though, at least for Cory, is that "these people are my friends."

It is notable that, amongst the friendships making New Abbey a reality, Cory points to the importance of his relationship with Nick Warnes, a Presbyterian leader with a heart for church planting and co-editor of *Starting Missional Churches*. His philosophy of church growth subverts that of "box store churches" and is rooted in Biology 101. "It's not about how big you can grow," Nick says, "but how much you can reproduce."[2] From that reasoning, Nick led his church to invest in New Abbey by offering a connection to the mainline and mentoring for how to secure funding. Cory goes so far as to say, "We would not have made it without Nick's friendship."

For a long time, the mainline church has been content to allow the janitor holding the broom to dictate how best to put on the parade.[3] In other words, the mainline strategy has been to give its top level leadership positions to those that keep things ordered and limit the mess. All the while the church, like a parade, begs to be a carousing affair where sirens are blasted and candy is strewn. Who will decide how to put on the mainline's parade in the twenty-first century? If it's the innovator, if it's people like Nick Warnes, the mainline might find more people like Cory marching in from other traditions and more churches like New Abbey making noise.

2. Nick Warnes, interview with author, June 29, 2015.

3. Merlin Mann's concept.

AMOS DISASA

Downtown Church
Columbia, South Carolina

In their book, *Starting Missional Churches*, Mark Branson and Nicholas Warnes advocate for developing leadership from within a context. They say, "a new church needs to be connected with the innovations of a local people."[4] As such, they go on to warn against the dangers of a church-starting strategy that drops experts into a neighborhood as if the merits of a well-developed strategy trump the cachet of a locally well-known individual. Amos Disasa, who started Downtown Church in Columbia, South Carolina, is evidence to that fact. Birthed in 2011, Downtown Church grew to over two hundred worshipers in the course of its first year and Amos attributes much of the church's fast growth to his familiarity with Columbia. "You not only have to communicate vision, but you have to build trust in your context. People already knew me."[5]

The Disasa family arrived in Columbia from Ethiopia 1983. He was just a boy then and, except for his college years at nearby Presbyterian College and seminary at Wake Forest, the city has been his home ever since. He served for several years at a large church in Columbia then decided to break off and start something of his own. Born from a love of the context and a dream for the church, Amos began his planting journey with a season of internal work. "I wrote a lot first," he says; "there were grants to write. But it was an exercise not just to get money; it forced me to think about the core values of the ministry. I had to answer that, so that was good." Amos knew the neighborhood from years living there and, through his reflective writing, began to better know how God was calling him to it.

Upon securing grant money from a variety of different denominational sources, Amos began his ground game. He was pragmatic in his approach. "You go to work," he said. "You have to get in front of a lot of people. You start and it's like selling insurance. You go to your circle of friends and tell them 'this' is what we're doing. Early on, it was about drinking coffee and beer with people. Every minute you're not doing that, you're wasting your time."

From the outside looking in, these looked like casual appointments, but there was nothing aimless about what he was doing. Those that met

4. Branson and Warnes, *Starting Missional Churches*, 20.
5. Amos Disasa, interview with author, May 20, 2015.

with Amos were offered a tangible hook and an invitation for immediate participation. "You have to give them something to buy into. Initially, for us, it was the launch team. We were looking for about thirty people who would commit to start the church. That's the only commitment they were making." Amos had a sense they had something when twenty-seven of the thirty were committed by the end of his first two months.

One of the first practical tasks for the launch team was to determine the meeting space for their fledgling project. Amos names establishing clarity about what constitutes a critical mass, what makes a space feel alive, as the number-one logistical "must-do" for a church start. He points out that

> Critical mass depends on space. You need to have 80 percent of maximum capacity or close to that every single Sunday. It has to look full because that's where you get your credibility. It doesn't matter how great the worship is or how good the preaching is, if nobody is in there, it's going to feel dead and people are asking "What is wrong with this church?" It's like a restaurant on a Friday night, the food could be great but if it's seven o'clock on a Friday and there is one person sitting at a table by themselves, it's unlikely that you are going to stick around and taste the food.

The Downtown Church launch team toured a number of worship spaces, tried out a few by actually holding worship in them, and landed on a renovated community building in the center of the city. They have been there ever since.

Today the church continues to grow with healthy attendance every Sunday. Worship services at Downtown Church are neither traditional or contemporary. Amos jokes, "at this point, worship is kind of, 'What Amos likes.'" The music is a blend of ancient music, rearranged traditional hymns, and re-appropriated modern music. In any given worship service, the community might sing something written by Fanny Crosby and later hear a song done by well-known artists Sufjan Stevens, Nickel Creek, or Death Cab for Cutie. "It's not about contemporary or traditional," Amos says, "it's whether or not you're believable."

When Amos looks back on the current work of this ministry, he offers a formula. "It is simple: leadership + money + patience + vision = a good start." But then he gives one final piece of direction by way of a surprising warning to anyone interested in starting new churches in the mainline. "The best measure of your faithfulness to the call is whether or not established churches consider you to be a threat. You will become an outsider in the institution that ordained you. If that doesn't happen, you will probably fail." In other words, if you are starting a new church and the churches you know can stomach what you're doing, you're probably not doing enough.

MIKE BAUGHMAN

Union Coffee
Dallas, Texas

When Mike Baughman was a kid growing up on the Jersey shore, he often woke up to the rotten-egg smell of the tide going out. The stench was courtesy of a marsh near his neighborhood. The marsh was also responsible for the stinging, green-headed flies that invaded everyone's back yards and the impenetrable mud that stuck to children's play clothes.

One day, when he was twelve, Mike asked his father why someone hadn't developed the marsh and spared everyone from its torment. To that, his father replied, "Yes, the marsh smells bad, it hurts sometimes, and it's messy. But, without the marshlands there'd be no life in the ocean, a lot less life in the air, and less life on the land." That day he learned an important lesson about life, faith, and ministry—when worlds meet, mess happens. When mess happens, there is a good chance that life, and that God, is around. It is from Mike's hope in the marsh-inspired promise of world's meeting that Union Coffee in Dallas, Texas, was born.

In the one world is Union's coffee consumers. It functions as a normal coffee shop with a lot of space for eating, working, and sharing conversation. There are even small conference rooms available for workshop leaders or businesses to rent. Mostly, though, just like other local coffee shops, they just do their best to offer a great coffee product in a comfortable atmosphere. Mike admits, "For most of our customers, we're nothing more than a great coffee shop that does generous things for the community; and we have great Wi-Fi and we're happy to provide that for them."[6]

Meeting that world is the world of Union Coffee as a worshipping community. It is the home for two unique worship gatherings per week and a platform for local community engagement. That said, it's not, as Mike puts it, a "Jesus Cafe or a hangout for über-Christians. Most of the people that worship with us are church refugees in some form or fashion. Most of

---

6. Mike Baughman, interview with author, June 30, 2015.

them left the church with their middle finger in the air behind them. The other half left the church because they were bored."

"Boring" is nothing new for the mainline. It is a moniker that is tough to avoid, what with all of the old hymns, played on old instruments, and old words, spoken by old men, from old perches. And yet, it was the, supposedly, boring and old United Methodist Church of the mainline that took the risk in investing in Union. Its commitment came, not just in money, but in relationships. Mike received support from one congregation, in particular, that provided startup capacity for Union. Before they had the bank account or support staff, this congregation made room for the startup to get on its feet. His thirty-person launch team was comprised of many members of pre-existing Methodist congregations. Finally, in a unique move for a church plant, Mike also gained the fellowship of a number of area small churches. He called them "covenant relationships" and they were established, first, to diffuse any feelings of competition. Second, he notes, "the reality is that most small churches don't have the funds, resources, or people to launch a new church. It was a way for them to experience that excitement, to hear stories of transformation, to have some of the pride in making it happen." Union is proof that small churches can be vital to the church planting movement and bring a seed of resiliency that many larger churches have never cultivated.

Small churches are not the only unlikely guests at Mike's planting party. From the very beginning, Mike regarded church refugees and skeptics as the primary developers of Union's worship services. He works on the principle that the people you attract to your worship will reflect your worship design team. "If you have a bunch of people that already really love Jesus," he says, "those are the people you are going to attract. The people that already love Jesus. But," he goes on, "if you have people on the team that are really nervous and sketchy about church, you will attract people that are nervous and sketchy about church." As a result, Union Coffee brings two distinct and compelling worship services per week and both are growing. The Tuesday service, in particular, now welcomes between fifty and sixty people per week and the average age of their worshipers is twenty-four years old.

How do they do it? As with the coffee shop itself, this worship service is dedicated to combining worlds of life and faith in making room for people and their relationships to grow. For starters, it is rooted in the ancient world. They call the service "*kuneo*," from the Greek word for worship, "*proskuneo*," which comes from the words "*pros*," meaning toward, and "*kuneo*," which means "kiss." Mike suggests that the worship is like a kiss, "something you anticipate, something that leaves you feeling different afterwards, something where you get to know somebody in a powerful way, and if it's a little awkward, that's OK too."

Second, the service is decidedly modern. Most of the music in the service is drawn out of the popular music world. While this may feel like anathema to the traditional church, the worship leaders at Union lean on a theology of God's omnipresence and the reality that pop music offers a more comfortable entry point for its population. It's not just the music though that provides the modern aura—Mike describes his preaching as "interactive" and they even leverage Twitter during announcement time. Have an announcement? Tweet it at them and they will read it during worship.

Finally, the service brings worlds together as it nods to tradition. The closing hymn, for instance, is always a traditional hymn. He explains that "one of the things we've learned is that the songs of the homeland are important to the refugee. We don't start there, but that's what we move toward." Clearly, worship at Union coffee was not designed to be cool, but congruent. Congruent with its roots, with its current population, with the theology of its leadership, and with the shape of its tradition.

Mike warns those that would follow his path: "Trail blazers take arrows. Some people will think that your innovative idea is amazing. Others will actively stand in the way of your success. Generally, it's the more established, powerful leaders who will stand in the way." For those that are called to it, though, the fruit is sweet. After all, these days Mike wakes up to a new smell—that of coffee—but in that smell, just like that of the marsh, there is a meeting of many worlds. It is where consumers meet community and skeptics meet tradition and, ultimately, it is where life happens.

BRINGING IT HOME

One of the many beautiful things Cory, Amos, and Mike model for the church is how they are committed to starting something else, while not leaving the old on the shelf or simply piling it on top of the old. Like with the widow's books, it takes a kind of spiritual respect and artfulness to be handed something old, something that deserves the dignity of being kept, and given a seat of honor—believing it to be of value, trusting it to be useful, even when it's not immediately clear why. And that is how it was with one book. One small book.

Years after I visited the widow, I readied myself to take communion to Elizabeth Rada.

She is seventeen years old on the day of this story and she is readying to leave for Texas for a last ditch dose of platelets and chemo, they call it a Hail Mary treatment. I assemble the communion kit—juice and crackers in a small wooden box—and look in my office for a small Bible to take along with me. I could only find big ones. Big, clumsy ones. I scan my shelves for something smaller and my hand comes across one small book from the widow's library. It is a *Book of Common Worship*, a tattered prayer book that most pastors have on hand for weddings, funerals, and pastoral visits. The widow's husband's is hardback and, as I open it, I notice that he has left a treasure of poems, Scripture verses, and ideas tucked inside. Flipping through, I find a piece of scrap paper. Scrawled on the paper are the verses I will share with Elizabeth and her family that day.

As she sits up in her hospital bed at A. I. DuPont Hospital for children, this is what I say. "As you head to Texas in the days ahead, remember the words of Isaiah chapter 55, verse 12." Then I read the scrawled handwriting from inside the book,

> You will go out in joy and be led forth in peace;
> the mountains and hills will burst into song before you,
> and all the trees of the field will clap their hands."

Several weeks later I am sure to include this as a passage that is read at Lizzie's funeral.

It is difficult to leave Elizabeth on that day because you never know, you just never know with cancer. But I say goodbye after a short visit; I have to, it is a Sunday night, and it is my turn to preach at the Sunday night service at Cokesbury village, a retirement community.

They are waiting for me at Cokesbury. They are waiting to have pre-worship dinner until I get there. The village's chaplain rises to greet me. She has invited a handful of residents to eat with us. Some of them I know well, some of them I don't know at all.

We sit down to eat at a rectangular table. We share small talk. My mind is at A. I. DuPont Hospital for Children. I pick at my food with my fork.

I lift my face. I look across the table, maybe for the first time. There she is. The widow. Sitting directly across from me. On this night. How is she here? Are my eyes deceiving me?

"Did you?" I ask her. "Are you the one that gave me books?"

"Yes," she says, "that was me."

I put my fork down. The table gets quiet. I tell her how I have just read aloud her husband's handwriting. The table is more quiet.

How she feels at the sound of these words, God only knows.

But I know about that book. I know how foolish I would have been to let it go.

CHAPTER 7

Matt and Nate

Evangelism

I first met Matt at an orientation for new counselors at Camp at the Eastward, where I had attended in some capacity, as camper or counselor, since I was in the third grade. He was from Connecticut and it was his first year there. We were introduced to one another by Dolores, the camp director and multi-faceted heart and soul of the place.

Dolores was, somehow simultaneously, the most loving and terrifying person any of her counseling staff had ever met. She usually wore an oversized camp T-shirt from years gone by, had a can of coke in one hand, and a half-burned-out cigarette in the other. She was the loudest singer at the campfire, the greatest hug on the toughest day, and the biggest smile at the closing ceremonies. Still, even if I knew it, I would not dare to reveal her age. I will only say that we knew when she was really getting serious when she popped her false teeth out just to get our attention.

The day she introduced me to Matt, she had her entire staff seated on wooden benches around well-loved and oft-marked wooden camp tables. She passed out papers with schedules and chore responsibilities. Then she gave the two of us our marching orders, "Get Cabin 9 ready! The two of you will be spending the summer in there together." Off we went, into the woods, to make sure the plywood floors were swept off and to check to be sure we had the right number of mattresses for the campers to come the next day.

After that, Matt told me he planned to take a drive to the nearest town for camp snacks and I watched him climb into his Chevy Suburban and roll up the camp road. A few minutes later I realized that I, too, needed to stock up on orange soda and snack cakes, so I pulled my car out and headed in the same direction up the perpetually bumpy Route 43, which spanned the thirteen miles to the nearest store in Farmington.

About halfway there I noticed a huge car along the side of road.

It was a black and red suburban.

There was Matt, sitting in the driver seat.

He had run out of gas.

I shook my head with an air of superiority and mumbled to myself, "Go figure. This flatlander has not even been here a day and I'm going to have to rescue him." I rolled down the window and invited him into my car and there we began what would be a really beautiful and rich friendship.

We were both barely twenty years old and planned to spend the next month with the rowdy campers in Cabin 9, but, we soon found out, we could not have been more different.

He was from an affluent New York City commuter town while my town could only boast a small candy store established on Tom and Dot Soule's front porch.

He was a philosophy major at a prestigious Presbyterian school and I was working through my fourth major at the local state University.

He had the finesse that comes with being a record-setting swimmer and I had all the nuance you would expect from a state champion wrestler.

He was a die-hard Yankee fan and my Red Sox had not won a World Series for eighty years, but who was counting?

Finally, I was a lifelong Christian whose parents faithfully bounced back and forth between the Presbyterians and the Pentecostals but Matt was, as he put it, "agnostic." I can clearly recall that somehow we managed to discuss all of this—hometowns, colleges, athletics, baseball, and faith— on that fateful ride to Farmington and back. I can also recall being very sure that God had intentionally put Matt in my way and, as such, that it was now my distinct privilege and calling to win him over, to convert him, and to make him into a disciple of Jesus Christ.

You can imagine how well that worked out.

There are a variety of foolish stories to tell on myself in my conquest to turn Matt's heart. There was the day he introduced me to New York City and I tried to manipulate him into helping me hand out WWJD bracelets to people in Time Square. Or the day that I led the camp staff meeting and, in front of everyone, asked if he would open with a spontaneous word of prayer. I can't count how many times I told him, one way or another, that I was concerned about his soul burning in hell.

The worst was the time that Matt lost his car keys and I said, "Let's pray that we find them." Then, upon saying "Amen," I sent an army of fifty kids and counselors to scour the field to find the keys. Go figure, they soon found them and, as I victoriously put them in his hand, I crowed, "See? The power of prayer."

The promise is perfect, but the people are not.

It has always been that way. From the days of Eden and Babel, when paradise and provision were not good enough, to the time of David who misunderstood God's grace for carte blanche to use the world as his personal playground, to the Romans who hung transcendence on a tree, to many of today's Christians, myself included, that wield the promise like a battle axe in a heroic attempt to hack people into some unnatural spiritual shape in the name of evangelism.

But then there are others, like the current Pope, who take a different approach to evangelism. After his election, Pope Francis preached, "We also sense our closeness to all those men and women who, although not identifying themselves as followers of any religious tradition, are nonetheless searching for truth, goodness, and beauty, the truth, goodness, and beauty of God. They are our valued allies in the commitment to defending human dignity, in building a peaceful coexistence between peoples and in safeguarding and caring for creation."[1] Not to be outdone by the Catholics, a like-minded approach to evangelism, one interested in meeting people instead of mutating them, can be found in a sprinkling of mainline Protestant ministries. The Slate Project, The Nave, The Garden Church, and the Big Gay Church show us what evangelism can look like when the church is open to doing something else.

---

1. "Address of the Holy Father Pope Francis," March 20, 2013.

JASON CHESNUT

The Slate Project
Baltimore, Maryland

Evangelism in the Online Neighborhood

With a flick of her wand, the Blue Fairy gives Pinocchio a mouth to speak and hinges on his wooden limbs so that he can dance. In his great excitement at this gift, Pinocchio makes the mistake of believing he is real. "To become a real boy," the Blue Fairy corrects Pinocchio, "you must prove yourself brave, truthful, and unselfish."[2] She knows that a little puppet can be alive without being real, and to be real there are certain, specific conditions that Pinocchio must meet. Sometimes the church falls into "Blue Fairy" syndrome when it assesses new creations in ministry. Does it meet our standards for legitimacy? Can we measure it in the way we always measure things? Yes, it is "alive," but is it "real"? Jason Chesnut, the Gepetto of the online ministry The Slate Project, hears the "Blue Fairy" interview regularly and he's surprising her with his answers.

Jason's work began through a generous investment by an ELCA (Evangelical Lutheran Church in America) congregation in Baltimore, Maryland. He took the three-year gig to create a new worshiping community with zero connections in the city, almost no plan, and a promise for very little outside oversight. In short, his horizon was a blank slate. So Jason began by doing things that interested him personally, spending most of his time creating original videos and social media platforms. His first month of evangelism was unique in that, instead of knocking on physical doors, he created virtual online meeting places.

For him, that was time well spent. He shares, "I was at Starbucks the other day and there were ten people in line and every single one of them was on their phone. In most places, that's decried. 'Look up,' they say, 'engage the world.' I just feel like they are engaging their world and I feel like it's my job to be on their radar, if they are on their phone all the time we should be where they are."[3]

While it is becoming trendy for churches to use words like "local" and "neighborhood," Jason is one of the few evangelists willing to go to the online "neighborhood" where so much of the world hangs out. His ministry

---

2. Disney, *Pinocchio*.

3. Jason Chesnut, interview with author, July 23, 2015.

is rooted in consistent and creative online content—every week, no matter what. This includes a blog, professionally-produced video, and compelling images. The Slate Project also hosts weekly Bible studies using hashtags on Twitter and digital disciplines in Advent and Lent using Facebook and Instagram. But, the "Blue Fairy" church still has to ask, "Is it real?"

Jason confronted some of that resistance by partnering with Jennifer DiFrancesco, a local Presbyterian minister, and Sara Shisler Goff, an Episcopal priest, in developing two weekly face-to-face gatherings. One is an ancient-future meal that mixes prayer, food, and candlelight with the digital age. The other physical meet-up is forthrightly monikered, "A Bible Study That (Hopefully) Doesn't Suck." Jason recognizes the importance of these get-togethers, but he is careful not to allow his online work to become a slave to them. "Overwhelmingly," Jason says, "churches create online content that points to their face-to-face gatherings. It's all about their face-to-face. If you're connecting with them online and you're not connecting face-to-face it's almost like it doesn't count."

But the online work of The Slate Project has counted. One woman credits Slate with helping her to become Christian again and inspiring her to go to seminary. Slate has a growing list of subscribers for its YouTube channel and a steady base of people reading the blog and sharing the content using social media. Also, Slate is there for those that need pastoral care but can't, for whatever reason, physically approach a pastor or church building. Jason explains, "I've ended up doing a lot of pastoral care online. People send us messages or tweet us. I'm constantly trying to engage that aspect so that those people are being heard. They may not feel comfortable coming in person and so, for them, what's powerful is being able to connect online." Finally, the Thursday night Twitter chat and Bible Study has established a regular following of twenty to thirty people and, unlike physical gatherings of any kind, it is truly open to anyone who wants to look in or even engage.

Jason's hope is that his creation can be a resource to churches with an eye for doing evangelism online. Some pastors are already using his videos as Bible study resources and sermon illustrations, but he hopes that church leaders will begin to consider the online world, not just as a starting point for future pew filling, but as a valid place to meet people and make transformative impact. Just by liking and sharing Slate's content, promoting the seasonal digital disciplines, and using the Slate hashtags, churches and leaders can begin to create an online ministry and reach out to the worldwide neighborhood.

Near the end of Pinocchio's great story, the puppet, like today's mainline church, lies dormant in a bed and is believed to be dead. But then, like magic, he lifts his human head and rubs his human eyes to see Gepetto crying at his bedside.

"Father," he says, "what are you crying for?"

Unfazed by the voice of the boy, Gepetto sobs, "You're dead! You're dead Pinocchio."

To which Pinocchio squeals, "No, I'm not. I'm alive. And I'm, I'm real."[4]

This is the kind of call that Jason Chesnut and Slate Project are making in the mainline church. This thing is alive and real. By joining them in evangelism in the online frontier, the mainline might hear other voices coming alive and feeling real too. Who knows? The church itself might be released from being quite so wooden.

RUTH ALLEN AND CRAIG MILANESI

The Nave
Somerville, Massachusetts

New Relationships through the Sharing of Space

A nave is defined as "the central part of a church building, intended to accommodate most of the congregation."[5] It is generally the place that church people go to sit in pews, receive communion, and hear a sermon. A non-church person might wander into a nave and come to wonder if they are trespassing. Not so for many who wander through the open doors of Clarendon Hill Presbyterian Church, in search of the "nave." The space communicates inclusion, vibrancy, and beauty. Credit the Nave Gallery for that.

Located in an arts-saturated pocket of the greater Boston area, the Nave Gallery is home to an association devoted to the use of art as a medium for expression and well-being. It is a place where local artists display portfolios, renowned virtuosos strut their stuff, and everything in between. There is no limit to their scope of media; the Nave has staged painters, sculptors, and musicians of all kinds. "Our priorities," writes Melissa Glick,

4. Disney, *Pinocchio*.
5. *Oxford Dictionary*, s.v. "nave."

a Nave member, "are community relationships and using the arts to influ-ence those who come into contact with it, to examine their own worlds."[6] It does all of this from a previously under-used room off the entrance of Clarendon Hill Presbyterian Church.

To the members of CHPC, as it would be for members of any church, that space was more than just another room. They remembered it as a place where adult education classes were held and committee meetings gathered. It was how they walked from one part of the building to another. Craig Milanesi, a member of the church, recalls how it was used as an intimate space for fellowship dinners or even to have worship when attendance was low. The space was never vital to the ministry of the church, but it did of-fer conveniences from time to time. To welcome the Nave Gallery meant giving up these conveniences and letting go of some memories, a difficult transition for any church. Craig says they put that task alongside an even greater one, "the church doesn't have a pre-entitled voice any more. We have to establish new ways to acquire one on the issues that matter to us."[7] So, in 2004, through the leadership of then pastor, Karl Gustafson, himself an artist active in the community, they made room for the Nave. And a choir of new voices are emerging from the walls of the church.

There are voices from the arts community. They tell important sto-ries of love lost, justice undone, hope found, dreams pursued, racism re-vealed, and desperation stifled. As might be expected, an entirely new way of accessing deep and honest human expression is elevated through the artistic work of the gallery, but, even more, a call for community help is being sounded. CHPC member Ruth Allen hails the gallery for its long-term commitment to the Somerville Homeless Coalition and the way it has engaged their church partner in a deeper outreach to their homeless neighbors. Together, the church and the gallery have garnered trust in each other and established a hard-earned reputation in the community for speaking out on major national and international issues of social justice. When protests flare in Ferguson or when missiles fly in the Middle East, the Nave and CHPC have a pre-existing platform for engaging the com-munity's mourning, discussion, and motivating action.[8]

There are also voices that come from the church to the arts com-munity. For most churches, the traditional holy seasons offer a time for

6. Glick, "Nave Gallery and Nave Annex a Project of Love."

7. Craig Milanesi, interview with author, June 11, 2015.

8. Ruth Allen, interview with author, June 23, 2015.

reconnection, a spiritual pick-me-up for those seeking or disassociated. CHPC has come to realize that the post-Christendom purge is shuffling the church calendar. Ruth Allen chuckles as she confesses that the busiest times of the CHPC year are not Christmas and Easter, but during Somerville Open Studios, a multi-day community-wide event that brings thousands of visitors to the city. She tells of a time when she was sitting at the gallery "and a woman came in before the show and she asked about the church and I told her that I was a member. Then she asked for a prayer request. She filled out a prayer card, we shared it with the deacons, and prayed for her on Sunday morning. That just felt like a really important connection." It might not be amidst Christmas trees and Easter lilies, and it might not be from the pulpit, but it is still critical witness and community care. It is an entirely different kind of evangelism than what the mainline is accustomed to, where a sincere sharing of the embodied gospel is an end unto itself with no self-serving strings attached.

While a few CHPC members attribute the church's commitment to the arts community as a reason for their initial interest, contributors and visitors of the Nave have not pivoted to join the church. There is no great windfall of new stewardship dollars rushing in as a result of the increased foot traffic. Put simply, evangelism and church growth are two different things and no amount of professional pressure on a pastor or other church leader to magically turn bodies in the building to people in the pews can change that. And yet, Ruth tells an important story of two flags that fly outside of the CHPC. One is the pride flag and "next to that we have the Nave flag up when they are open. I always get a rush when I walk by and I see that flag. It shows that the church is alive and kicking." A church that unlocks its nave may not be the answer to ensuring its institutional future, but it might just be to reestablishing its prophetic kick.

ANNA WOOFENDEN

The Garden Church
San Pedro, California

Evangelism as Intentional Presence in the City

We were garden people at the start. As described by Genesis, it is in a garden that we first learn who we are as human beings. We felt the dirt underneath our nails, hid in the grass, avoided a snake, stood around a tree and, ultimately, tasted its fruit. Eden, which comes from an Aramaic word meaning fruitful and well-watered, represented a special place for God's people to grow and be about growing, separate from everything else.[9]

Banished from Eden a long time ago, we humans have spent an existence doing our best to create new "Edens." We long for a safe place, someplace separate from the chaos, to be fruitful and taste living water. It is a place where we can expose our vulnerabilities, wrestle with our shortcomings, and come to terms with our innocence or lack thereof. Once in a while we even succeed at doing this, but we don't call it a garden, we call it the church. Except for Anna Woofenden, she calls it The Garden Church.

The garden is a natural home for Anna. She grew up on a homestead and spent much of her childhood playing in the dirt. Her heart for ministry is rooted in her awareness that the digging and planting that she experienced as normal and formative is not a reality for many of today's children, especially in urban and under-served areas of the world. Her ministry seeks to rectify that in one little corner of the planet. "One of the things that drives me," she says, "when I look at the world and agriculture, I see that more and more and people are just consumers of food. There is a disconnection from food, God, and community."[10] And so, after years of working in the denominational halls of the church, followed by a season of seminary and training, she joined her passion with the Swedenborgian Church to sow something new.

The work began with a nationwide search to locate a plot of land in a community dealing with food insecurity needs. Ultimately, Anna landed in a vacant lot in San Pedro, California and began the work of reaching out to the community. The lot sits at a crossroads, of sorts, at the literal intersection of poverty and affluence. She describes how they first walked the streets of the community for three months and how "that was incredibly important because we got to know people and establish that they were seen by us as valued and human." From its first moments, evangelism, for The Garden Church, was not a conquest project but a creation one. They were to be about creating space for new plants to be cultivated and new fruits to be harvested, and especially, new relationships to be born.

"The garden is a leveling place," Anna preaches, "everyone's hands get dirty." There in the dirt, God's people meet one another, often coming from

---

9. *The Oxford Dictionary of the Jewish Religion*, s.v. "Eden."

10. Anna Woofenden, interview with author, July 2, 2015.

very disparate places and life experiences, in their most ancient task. There, just as God came to the *adamah*[11] to create the *adam*[12] from scratch, God comes to those in the dirt to create something new and alive in those relationships. These days, The Garden Church holds a weekly worship service that includes garden work, traditional liturgy, and a communal meal. It is establishing a venue for planting and peacemaking workshops. It is offering an inviting atmosphere for the community to come and listen to musical guests and just be still to pray. Yet, in all of this programming, there lives a recognition that God is the first and best evangelist and ours is the work of making just enough relational mess for God to have something to till.

As Anna finds traction with her diverse community, and word gets out about it, she fears that the temptation for mainline churches will be to launch garden offshoots of their own. Some churches are already situating community gardens on or near their property in an evangelistic effort. Anna worries, "some churches assume, 'If I put a vegetable garden in my front yard, my church will be saved.' I don't think saving churches is the work of The Garden Church. I think it is a canvas to work with the important question—'How do we completely reimagine church in this generation?'" Reimagined, it might be that churches have many people passing through with only a few staying for good, it might be that churches put a priority on befriending neighbors, and it should be that churches become places, as Anna puts it, "to feed and be fed." In other words, if the primary motivation of your evangelism (gardening or otherwise) is saving your church, it probably isn't evangelism.

Far from Eden, we find another garden growing at the very end of the Bible. Described in the final chapter of Revelation, the Heavenly City boasts a garden that includes the tree of life, open gates, abundant light, and flowing water. If you ask Anna, that is the kind of garden that her church hopes to emulate. "The Garden of Eden is separate," she says, "but in the Heavenly City the garden is right in the middle." At the end of all of this, we will, once again, be garden people. So, while no garden is going to save a local church, a vision of the Heavenly City, where the garden is located—not as separate—but firmly in the center of all the facets of life, might shape our ministry for what is ahead for now and forever.

11. The Hebrew word for dirt.

12. Literally, "dirt person."

HOLLY CLARK-PORTER

Big Gay Church
Wilmington, Delaware

Evangelism with the Queer Community

The week that Holly and her wife, Kaci, were ordained as Presbyterian ministers in a joint service at First and Central Presbyterian in Wilmington, Delaware, they received national attention from the media. Not only were they the first same-sex couple to be ordained in the same Presbyterian service, the ordination took place only days after the denomination formally approved its ministers to officiate same-sex marriages. The wave of publicity was high and they were, willfully or not, along for the ride. For some, that made the Clark-Porters a bull's-eye for bigoted dart throwing. The darts came in many forms; she remembers receiving full copies of the book of Romans, messages laced with foul language, and a comment in an online piece that called her wife "the spawn of Satan with reptilian eyes and dark skin." She remembers watching Kaci's family read that comment and says, "That was the worst. It was a bad moment. For all of us."[13]

She is right. It was a bad moment for all of us and it was an especially bad moment for those that identify as "church." However, it is from this nasty history with religious fundamentalism that Holly is motivated to offer the queer community a "love beyond welcome" and the "apology they never got" through the Big Gay Church. At first, the name suggests this is a ministry begging to *provoke* ill will, but Holly tells another story. "The more I put the name out there, the more I saw the hidden queer voices drawn to the church." It is a provocative ministry, to be sure, but instead of acrimony, it is provoking access.

To Holly's surprise, harsh critique of her ministry is not limited to those that, as she puts it, "dare not look me in the eye for fear of catching 'it.'" It is also "the academic, queer, Christian, trained community," she laments. "They are all on a different page, many are doing work with people who are already feminists; they are working with people who already know what cisgender means. But the people that I am working with, they don't know about themselves, never mind this whole community they are supposedly involved in." Periodically snubbed even by the people she identifies with

13. Holly Clark-Porter, interview with author, July 2, 2015.

most, Holly still presses on. For her, this work is a calling, not something she sought out for liberal accolades, but because God pushed her into it.

When she began her work in Delaware as a resident evangelist with F.I.R.S.T. (Freeing the Imagination of the Recently Seminary Trained), she hoped to start a church in a trendy section of her city. She drew up plans and strategized with her support team. She followed all the best advice, but a year into that endeavor, she recognized the effort was stalling for a variety of reasons and decided to recalibrate. Over and again she found herself ministering, mostly informally but always meaningfully, to those navigating issues of sexual identity. "Maybe we should just start the Big Gay Church," she mused one day. Then, before she could stop it, the name and premise stuck.

The BGC meets monthly for worship and regularly for studies. Beyond that though, the ministry is a lifeline to local moms and dads who need pastoral support in the midst of their teen's coming out and offers biblical re-literacy in the face of a queer person's shaming by a religious family member. "My ministry," Holly specifies, "seems to be with people who are on the outskirts and who have family that they cannot come out to."

Her constituency doesn't stop at the boundaries of her neighborhood. She has a vital online ministry and is leading workshops on queer issues and speaking at corporate events. She describes a time at a health care forum when a gay orderly confessed how he feels like he's "less gay" because he doesn't know how to dress or never wears the right shoes. Another nurse raised her hand and shared how she worries about losing survey points if she reveals her orientation. "I stay silent when asked about my husband or I tell them about my pretend husband." Some might try to change these folks, to win them to the sort of "normal" sexuality that they grew up with and think the Bible supports.[14] Others might try to teach them, to win them to the right way of being queer. Holly does neither. She stops to listen, she gives them her time, and offers a dose of authentic kindness. She knows that the best evangelism has less to do with winning someone else to your idea than it does with turning yourself over to what God has in store.

Holly is accustomed to turnover. The call to ministry turned her over from a blossoming career in politics. When she married Kaci she turned from being under-the-radar to lightning-rod status. Her ordination turned her over from a harmless queer upstart to an important voice on a national

14. For those wishing to engage this topic in a scholarly and accessible way, consider reading *Homosexuality and the Christian Community* by Choon-Leong Seow.

stage. As that voice is heard, she is finding more and more people leaning in. "What's going on?" they ask her. "How can we pray for you?" The churches she visits are the most curious and helpful. "Even in some of the smaller, older churches," she says, "they are some of the best support." Maybe they were always that way, but maybe she is turning them over too.

BRINGING IT HOME

Evangelism is an ugly word in the mainline, but it doesn't have to be. Evangelism doesn't have to be an opportunistic endeavor where non-Christians are won by the "church." It can be opportunistic, but instead of an acquisitional opportunity, it can be an opportunity in giving ourselves over to someone else. This is, after all, what God did in Jesus. In this version of evangelism, we don't get to boast of souls saved, hearts won, or even members gained. But, when we "Do Something Else" with evangelism, what we get is friendship. And that is enough. It is enough for us. It is enough for God to use to do something more.

Over and against all of my Christian immaturity, Matt and I are friends. No, we are brothers. I know that he loves me and he knows that I love him. So, almost twenty years after that first day we met at camp, when his three-year-old daughter, Maia, was diagnosed with Leukemia, my heart was broken. So much so that I shared it with my congregation who did what a good church does; it kept them in prayer and sent a thoughtful care package. He wrote this to me after receiving a package of cards, letters, pencils, and quilts from the congregation:

> Thanks so much, man. I swear, I'm 39 years old and I'm still learning what small and simple words mean. Like the word "gift." This experience has certainly humbled me, and more importantly it has opened us to the beauty of the world. It is so easy to be jaded—easy for me. But I swear, I have had moments of joy throughout this, mostly rooted in the reminder that there is so much more that unites us rather than divides. So much love, and it is everywhere. Love has literally knocked on my door and came to us when we needed it.
>
> Thank you and your family and anyone else who might have contributed. You should see how she smiles when we get a card in mail. Her face seems to relax, she forgets the ache in her bones and the struggles of the day, and she feels the warmth of love. I know it, and that's the gift: easing my child's pain, healing Maia's illness.

And I really believe that this treatment will heal her, but it's your love and our community that will help her become whole. So now I'm thinking a real gift is something that can't possibly be paid back. It can't be exchanged or put a value on.

The gift is a sense of worth, a dialogue, where everyone benefits.

Blahblahblah. Love ya, man. Good night.

Somewhere in there, Matt sounds like Pope Francis. Somewhere in there Jason, Ruth, Craig, Anna, and Holly are applauding. Somewhere in there is the true sound, the beautiful ring of evangelism.

CHAPTER 8

Yarn Ball

Outreach

It was the final night of the mission trip. Counting the adult chaperones, there were thirty of us in the dormitory lounge. Some of us sat on the floor, others sprawled out on wooden chairs, and the lone couch was crammed with approximately two-too-many teenagers. One of the older teenagers held a jumbo-sized ball of yarn in her hands. She explained that "Yarn Ball" was the traditional way to close the church mission trip. The teenagers leaned forward in excitement; many of them had done this before. The older teenager then told us that the purpose of Yarn Ball was to pass the yarn to someone that made an impact on us in the past week and tell them why they were so special. After we affirmed someone, we were to hold the end of the yarn and pass the unraveling ball to them so they could do the same, and so on. The effect of all of this holding and passing, back and forth across the circle, was a huge web of yarn meant to symbolize our new web of church relationships.

It was my first summer as a pastor and one of my first experiences with this church so I was mostly an observer during this activity. But I remember reflecting, "So this is what the final night of a mission trip is like on this side of things." I always wondered. Up until this moment, I only knew the other side of mission trips.

Growing up as a recipient of mission efforts, I always just accepted that we were someone else's project. Even as a young child I understood that these church people were generous, but I also felt used. It was as if my home, humble as it was, transitioned for a week to become their worksite, photo studio, and giggle palace. All of it was tolerated though, not because they brought great workmanship (though some did) but because they brought money. Without their money for materials, the necessary improvements would wait another year and another year after that.

This is not news for most churches helping those in need. Those invested in outreach, mission trips or any other kind, are well aware of the role of money, not just in facilitating projects, but in reinforcing the power structure. Givers use money, consciously and subconsciously, to keep a firm and comfortable distance between "us" and "them." Dollars are like a firecracker to the mission field, they can make something exciting happen or they can blow up in your hand. Which is why, even if money is necessary for outreach, it must be assigned its proper place in the hierarchy of serving, far below genuine relationships, not just with one another (as elevated by yarn ball), but with those being served.

When outreach is done well, it is built on a theology of service that gets engrafted into the personality of the church. Essentially, it helps a church move past the anthropocentric (us-centered) idea of mission as the way we, "the powerful," give monetary benevolence to you, "the needy"; and it shepherds the community into a real theocentric (God-centered) acting out of mission as a means through which God brings everyone, all of us being "needy," into real relationship with God and with one another. As these holy friendships are brought to depth we find God showing up, unshackling our spirits, and reshaping our lives toward an embodiment of the kingdom that has come near. Put simply, the church does something else in outreach by moving from a hand-out ministry, past a hands-on one, to one that values the hand-in-hand.

As sacred and authentic as these experiences of incarnational community can be, churches struggle to embrace it as real mission, like they suppose monetary benevolence is, for at least two reasons:

1. Many church folks have a difficult time conceding that money can't fix what they think it can.

2. Many church folks have a difficult time admitting that they are among the needy.

Most people don't make this shift on their own. Some grow old and never make it at all. Which is why a church's commitment to an outreach program that insists on legitimate, relational experiences where a person is led to invest in those unlike themselves, not just with their work, but even with their intimacy, is so essential. This kind of relational outreach is modeled in the ministries of Chip Graves, Becca Gillespie-Messman, and Margaret Kelly.

CHIP GRAVES

Trinity Episcopal Church
Huntington, West Virginia

Metrotheology

"A priest, a prostitute, and her fiancé . . . "

It all started like a bad joke.

Chip Graves, rector at Trinity Episcopal in Huntington, West Virginia, remembers it this way: "The church was well-to-do, reserved, and 120 percent white. I kept rereading the Beatitudes and felt like we needed to go broader. I was praying that we could somehow open our doors to those that are not like us."[1] Everywhere Chip went he told people about his prayer. He chatted up the restaurant managers. He gabbed with the gas station attendant. He talked to city officials and caught the ear of the city mayor, a Trinity parishioner. He never asked for money or special favors, just advice. Finally, it was when he shared with the local hospice executive that he was directed to his best connection. "She has questionable past," he was told. "She's been in prison. She'll cuss a bit, but she's powerful and she might be the key to what you need."

And so that is how a priest, a former prostitute, and her fiancé launched a ministry together.

Father Chip asked her what she needed to help get the word out about a new helping ministry at his church and she told him, "500 flyers." The next day she came back to get 500 more. Within weeks, Trinity Episcopal had The Gathering, a mid-week dinner for the homeless that included a brief Episcopal worship service and anywhere from thirty to fifty attendees. Today that ministry has a regular attendance of over 150 per week and an ecumenical volunteer base that includes parishioners from six different churches. Like many pastors, Chip had a vision; but unlike most, Chip let

---

1. Chip Graves, interview with author, May 19, 2015.

the vision get out and then, with hopeful tenacity, he kept letting it out until something clicked.

It started like a joke, but its work is dead serious. The city of Huntington has a troubling recent history in engaging the homeless population. In 2008, the city controversially purged the Ohio River Bank of "Tent City." One homeless man, "Little Larry," was quoted at that time, "Huntington should address the homeless problem instead of moving around. The city makes them subhuman like they are less than everybody else." In the same report "Speedy," another homeless man predicted, "Tear it down once, it's going to start right back up again. Watch."[2]

Speedy's notion proved to be prescient and in September of 2013, Tent City was back and Huntington city officials were at it again. The city authorities attempted to be fair about it, but ultimately officers told everyone living in the area that they could no longer be staying there after a week, and everything left behind would be thrown away. It was into that kind of disruptive atmosphere that Chip led his church to start The Gathering in January of 2014.

Since then, the program has expanded to include "River City Ministry," that offers another meal on Saturday mornings which is often followed by another support ministry. Medical students from nearby Marshall University have provided healthcare, a shoe manufacturer has delivered shoes to the homeless, and the local clothing bank has joined the effort. Recently the outreach has expanded to include a drug addiction ministry, youth education, and a fine arts program. Packaged together, Chip calls the multifaceted ministry effort, "Metrotheology," partly because, in all of this, the same city government that once took a heavy handed approach is now, through his contextual leadership, chipping in.

As helpful as all of this sounds, this notion of outreach is falling out of vogue in the mainline. The best illustration of the criticism comes from Richard Lupton's book, "Toxic Charity," where he stresses, "giving to those in need what they could be gaining from their own initiative may well be the kindest way to destroy people."[3] He also encourages churches to recalibrate their outreach to "develop a dependency free zone."[4]

What Lupton fails to understand is that the work of the church is not to create better transactional relationships. It is tempting to understand

2. Seaton, "Huntington WV Riverfront Homeless Evicted from 'Tent City.'"

3. Lupton, *Toxic Charity*, 4.

4. Ibid., 101.

outreach that way. It allows the powerful to remain distant know-it-alls, while the powerless scurry to fall in line with the elitist's program. It is tempting, but it isn't true to the gospel. Instead of creating better trans-actional relationships, the best outreach elevates transformational ones. It should, indeed, cost people to receive free clothes at the clothing bank, or free food at the food closet, or free shelter at the housing ministry, but it shouldn't cost them money just because the "haves" know what's best for the "have nots." Instead, it should cost them their story; it should cost all of us an investment in relationship.

Through Metrotheology, Chip Graves, Trinity Episcopal, and the City of Huntington are creating an atmosphere for these kinds of relationships. He says, "these folks are hungry for attention and they are hungry for a voice. There is no place else where someone is asking, tell me your story." What's more, the relational benefit has been mutual. While Chip admits that much of the church membership was skeptical of the initial effort, in the past three years, Trinity's membership participation in outreach has tri-pled, their weekly attendance has doubled and their pledges have increased over 30 percent. People are being fed and nourished, the city's posture is being transformed, the church is growing, and humans are being human to one another. That is outreach and that is no joke.

MARGARET KELLY

Saint Paul Synod of the Evangelical Lutheran Church of America
Saint Paul, Minnesota

Shobi's Table

On the outside it looks like a regular calzone, but Shobi's pockets are dif-ferent. Margaret Kelly, the pastor and head foodie of Shobi's table in Saint Paul, Minnesota, can send you a list of ingredients, but the recipe for what makes the pocket special lies beyond the dough and filling. Whatever it is, when Margaret arrives near Payne and Maryland Avenues on Thursdays at 11 a.m., there is always a line forming.

Maybe the secret is not quantitative (precision with ingredients) but qualitative (direction of intention). Before the pockets hit the street where they are handed out free of charge, they pass through a gauntlet of care. Sometimes that comes by way of a partner congregation. Part of Margaret's ministry is to connect churches with her outreach. She describes how, "we go into a congregation, often a Wednesday evening, and they provide us with a group of workers and we come in and show them how to cook the meal with us."[5]

Her leadership crew consists of people from all walks of life. Some are "Catholics who got excited" she says. Others come from the margins where the pockets will go. Margaret stresses the importance of this because "now we have traditional Lutherans who want to try something, want to do something different. But, in it, they get to hear Gary's story about drug abuse and Noah's of being homeless and Candy's about trying to graduate high school. But there's no pressure, cause we're just rolling out dough." The group shares some of the pockets as their meal and sends the rest to be given out on Thursday.

In no way discounting the work with local churches, Margaret explains that most of Shobi's pockets are made on Thursday morning. Her team arrives at around 9 a.m. to begin a rowdy time of rolling out the dough and cooking. She calls that their "call to worship and coffee hour" where they are loud and obnoxious but take time to talk about what they will do on the street. Once their truck is freighted with food, they make their way to their regular location and everyone gets down to business. Candy manages the window, others sit in the truck and wrap food, and Margaret mingles with the congregation gathered. While the pockets are passed out, she prays with them and, just before noon, leads a brief lectionary-based worship service. They close every week with Holy Communion where Margaret has had people tell her, "That's the first time I've had communion in twenty-five years."

Margaret's work on that street mirrors that of a good pastor on Sunday morning, even if the people she shepherds are likely to see a church sanctuary as off-limits for them. She says, "I check in with people. We see mostly the same people every week. They say, 'Pastor can I tell you what's going on?' They are hungry to be known, recognized, remembered and just treated like a human. That's what I spend my time doing." For her, pastoral care begins with listening, remembering what she was told the week before, and sometimes being angry alongside people. She wears her collar and says it communicates, "I am an authority figure and you are worth my time."

Margaret has a background in food service, missionary ministry, and social work, so this call is a unique fit for her. That said, she did not initiate

5. Margaret Kelly, interview with author, June 24, 2015.

Shobi's table. Her predecessor established relationships with local congregations and her Lutheran Synod. After all of the paperwork and denominational negotiation, it was established as a three-year pilot project to explore to see if something might blossom. In many instances, this kind of exploration is directed at questions of independent viability. In this case Margaret concedes they will never be 100 percent self supporting, and yet the Synod and churches remain excited about what she is doing. Margaret says that the governing bodies recognize the plight of those ministries serving the impoverished. Like with the Shobi pocket, the measure of success for any outreach ministry is found, not in the quantitative, but the qualitative.

My friend Bill Perkins, another saint for those that live on the street, once spoke of the danger of using quantitative metrics in assessing the outreach of his ministry at Friendship House in Wilmington, Delaware. As he reflected on a string of sub-zero degree days in his city, he shook his head and said, "This week my metric is keeping people alive and giving them hope." Often times, funding agencies see things a different way. They look for numbers to inform their disposition and use words like "efficiency" and "competence" to determine future disbursements.[6] Instead of bending to the demands of the metric monster, Margaret echoes Bill's tone as she encourages those in outreach to "listen to the Holy Spirit. Trust the Holy Spirit."[7]

The name for Shobi's Table comes from an obscure story at the end of Second Samuel. The story goes that after Shobi's brother, Hanun, was defeated and deposed by David, Shobi became King of Ammon. At that point, Shobi had every reason to despise David and every motivation to return the violent favor. And yet, on the day when David's troops wander near to Shobi's land, even as they are exhausted and vulnerable, Shobi sets a nourishing feast before them. It is a story of hospitality and outreach even when it doesn't make sense. As it was with Shobi, as it is with Shobi's Table, the best outreach rarely makes sense at first glance, but is, instead, a taste of the feast to come.

6. Jesus did not use these words.

7. Jesus used these words.

BECCA GILLESPIE-MESSMAN

Trinity Presbyterian Church
Herndon, Virginia

Lunch for the Soul

Just before Dr. Thomas Gillespie retired from his twenty-one-year term as president at Princeton Theological Seminary, he gave a small group of would-be ministers three pieces of advice in finding their first call. First, look for a church that you can love and will love you in return. Second, if it suits you, stay close to home. That is, the task of ministry is difficult enough and being near your extended family will be of great help. Finally, take your time. Don't be the upstart that needs to make everything happen in the first year or two of your ministry.

Becca Gillespie-Messman heard that advice. She found a loving congregation that she could love in return, she found it close to home, and she had every intention of taking her time. Only it didn't work out that way. At her second ever meeting of the church session, the board took up a discussion around the newly hatched and politically controversial day laborer center in town and she found herself in the middle of it. "I think," one elder said, "we need to go to the day laborer site and invite them to come to our church for lunch and I think our new associate pastor should lead that because she speaks Spanish."

Becca tried to catch her breath. Then another elder spoke up with concerns for the wear and tear on the building. A different one chimed in with a resistance to ignite the political firestorm. One feared for the health of the pre-school and wondered out-loud if parents would feel comfortable sending their kids to a church if there were people "like that" there. Then the room started spinning with the Spirit and Becca remembers that "this key lady started crying and she said, 'I don't think I would want my kids to go to a church that would not have people 'like that' there.'"[8] Things got quiet and the session voted. It was unanimous in support of the first "Lunch for the Soul" (LFTS) and Becca, with some fear and trembling, was off and running.

They began by partnering with another local church, Riverside Presbyterian, but, even still, they thought they could keep the program small; so small maybe, that nobody would even notice they were there. "It wasn't

8. Becca Gillespie-Messman, interview with author.

the launching of a program," they told themselves. "It was an experiment. So don't be afraid." In a way, they were right. The first time they drove their mini-van to the center they were met by eighty curious faces, but only four took their invitation to come. For weeks they continued with the lunch and for weeks their guests could be accommodated with only one table to set up. After a few months, they grew to a cozy little program where a dozen or more guests gathered at noon on Wednesdays for food and Bible study. Everything was manageable at Lunch for the Soul, until the economy crashed and the day center closed.

The good folks at Trinity assumed that, with the day center gone, Lunch for the Soul was gone with it. That notion evaporated quickly. With fewer workers in the field, more were flocking to the fellowship hall. Soon, volunteers for LFTS were serving as many as two hundred people and the weight of the effort was spread out. Local restaurants and coffee shops came through with food donations. They partnered with other local congregations. Church small groups took turns hosting. Members of the Spanish speaking community were enlisted to help with crowd management. It was an enormous program and Becca acknowledges "we would not have been poised to do that if we had not done the little thing beforehand."

Spirit-led outreach ministry has a way of pushing the church past what it is prepared for and formally approved. C. S. Lewis says that God is like a good dentist in this way. He remembers how, as a child, he would wait as long as he could to tell his mother of a toothache. "I knew those dentists," Lewis wrote. "I knew they started fiddling about with all sorts of other teeth which had not yet begun to ache. Our Lord is like the dentists. If you give him and inch, He will take an ell. Once you call him in, he will give you the full treatment."[9] With a God like this, you know you are getting outreach right when it has the church opening so wide that all the ivories, ready or not, are being picked at and restored.

That is what is happening at Trinity. Becca remembers how the church first approached the issues brought to light by the day center. "We did what most churches do," she said, "we had a Sunday school class and a few people went and talked about it." This sort of attending to contemporary issues by way of workshops and webinars is the kind of engagement that allows the church to pretend it cares, without having to open up and be given a spiritual X-ray and plaque removal treatment. It allows the church to turn

---

9. Lewis, *Mere Christianity*, 201–2.

matters of life and death into cerebral projects and avoid the real work, not just of doing—but of being spiritually undone.

Now though, for Trinity, the work of LFTS is transformational. Becca recalls how an early detractor of the program came to serve with his small group. He looked on as the community ate and worshiped together. After the service, during the small group debrief, he shared, "You all know what I think about this kind of thing. But if our church was half as excited to come to church as these guys are, we would not be talking about decline in the mainline." The next Sunday he tracked Becca down and gave her a huge hug. Something changed for him.

Things are changing for Becca too. When someone connected to LFTS is imprisoned or hospitalized or even found behind a dumpster, she is called. She has done funerals for men killed by way of machete. She is being drawn into housing policy and educational program discussions. "It gets real if you hang in there with people on the edge," Becca says. Then again, most people that get into ministry want to do real things. For that matter, most people that come to the church, come because they want to do real things. With all of the recent talk about religious disaffiliation, maybe it's time to consider that the church just isn't giving the people anything to get excited about, anything substantial to get them to open up wide. Maybe it's time to get real. Ready or not.

BRINGING IT HOME

It is now ten years since that Friday night in the dormitories when I first learned how to play "Yarn Ball." During those ten years I have led mission trips to Maine, Costa Rica, Virginia, and South Africa. I spent time in inner city Wilmington with homeless men and under-served children. I read and speak extensively on the topic of mission, the missional church, and mission trips. After all of this, I am happy to report that I still think "Yarn Ball" is missing something.

The activity reminds me of what C. Peter Wagner calls "'koininitis': where interpersonal relationships become so deep and so mutually absorbing they can provide the focal point for almost all church activity and involvement."[10] Koininitis is relationship without the mission, it is the anti-mission.

---

10. Van Engen, *God's Missionary People*, 92–93.

If church teams must engage in a game to close out a mission trip or any other service project, I propose a new one. In this new, metaphorical game all the members of the team will sit in a circle, just like in "Yarn Ball." Then they will take three huge steps backward, providing room for those they met while on the trip or outreach event. The homeowners and homeless will be there, the hungry folks will attend, the church folks will be included, space will be made for the local storeowner, the boy that pumps the gas, and the little girl that watches from across the street.

Once the circle is complete, the group will stand in silence, and they will look each other in the eyes as an expression of mutuality, hospitality, and welcome. After a period of time, someone will pull out a ball, not a yarn ball, but an enormous ball of copper wire. One person will hold the heavy ball and pray for someone in the group, asking God to be present with them in every corner of their suffering and every second of their joy. That person will hold the end of the wire and pass it to the person that they prayed for, giving them a chance to pray for someone else, and so on, and so forth.

After everyone is given their chance to pray, there will be a huge web of this conductive material. Then, in one motion, as one community, they will lift their conductive web to the sky and pray for the miracle of mission. They will pray for our missionary God to charge the relational mission field with so much life-giving power that it unmasks every reality that exists outside the Lordship of Christ. Revealed will be the true essence of the entire experience, not a patched roof, not a repaired porch, not a painted house, but a passionate pursuit for something no less than the communal sharing in the electricity of God's life. Then our new community will be offering more than charity or benevolence as outreach. It will be doing something else, something beautiful and sincerely missional. And, through it, the whole of us, will be a little more alive.

CHAPTER 9

The Business of Life

Church Enterprises

Most regular churchgoers are unaware of how many curious things happen at church buildings during the work week. One ordinary Wednesday at my church a gas main broke and the authorities were rushed in by fire truck with all kinds of serious gear. The condition of the building was so dangerous, in fact, that we had to evacuate the craft group. One ordinary Monday, the entire pastoral staff became convinced that there was a squirrel stuck in the wall of the office building. Looking back, I'm not sure why we were so terrified, we were not the one stuck in the wall.

Then there was this one ordinary Thursday. If you were me on that one ordinary Thursday afternoon, you would've been walking through the building from the church library to the administration office. You would've been in a rush to get where you were going. You would've been in a rush because you were late for a church meeting. Your heart-rate would've been elevated because you hate being late for anything, but you would've been especially obsessive about being punctual and prepared for all meetings of church business. You would've been desperate to be seen as a bona fide professional, after all.

On this one ordinary Thursday, you would've been crossing through the eerily quiet and usually abandoned third floor and, like me, you would've barely noticed a disheveled young woman standing at the water fountain getting a drink. She would've been a complete stranger to you and, with her nest of hair and the streaks on her face, completely out of place in your tidy little church house. As curious as that might've been, you might've passed by her still because, after all, you would've been a pastor and you would've had a hearty portion of church business on your plate.

It was several years after this event—one we'll come back to later—that I started to consider how to find some perspective in attending to church business. It is sad, at least to me, that being in the church business is quite like being in any other business. It can be competitive and demanding. It can be overwhelming at times. It can make you, as it made me, wonder why you got it into the church in the first place.

Which is what made my experience of farming a pumpkin patch with Dick such an important season of my ministry. I'll never forget that summer. It was the year his wife, Barbara, died. We planted the seeds in the early spring, she was diagnosed with cancer in the late spring, and she was gone by mid-summer. Through all of that, one afternoon every week, I drove up to their "Bittersweet Farm"[1] to tend to our sizable pumpkin patch.

When we set out, our plan was to grow a monstrous crop; the goal was to have enough pumpkins to give one to every child at the church's annual fall festival. He warned me of the work ahead, but acquiesced to planting ten or so long rows of pumpkin seeds.

On my very first day of work on our project, I showed up a few minutes late, proudly wearing a brand new straw hat. Dick looked at my ridiculous getup and then at his watch and shook his head. Within seconds he had me up on the tractor. Even though I had never done so before, Dick wasted no time in setting me off to moving the levers and tilling the ground.

He showed me how to keep the tractor straight and he warned me not to hit Barbara's peonies planted perilously at the end of the row. For the record, I only nicked them one time, but figured she wouldn't notice. I was wrong.

It's funny, when you farm, you start caring about things you never really cared about before. A summer with those pumpkin hopes revealed that to me. When you farm, you start caring about the flowers that are on the plants. You start caring about the rain and you hope for rain and *how* it rains even matters to you. You, all of a sudden, start caring about the moon and what the moon is doing and how dirt looks. When do you ever care about how dirt looks?

I wish I could say that the harvest was some sort of heartwarming success in a season of heartache for Dick and for our church, but no amount

1. Yes, this is the actual name of the farm.

of hard work and good sentiment could overcome the devastating effects of the late summer hurricane that drowned the land. Not all was lost, though, at least for me. Because that summer, one afternoon every week, I did something else. I moved soil around and I planted things and pulled things from the ground and put a sharp hoe in the dirt. One afternoon every week I was not a pastor in the business of the church, I was a servant in the business of life. What a shame that those roles had become for me, and have become for many, so mutually exclusive. Part of what makes the ministry profiles to follow so beautiful is that, while so many pastors struggle to keep ministry from becoming business, Katie, Nikki, Matt, and Jen have turned business into ministry.

KATIE RENGERS

The Abbey
Birmingham, Alabama

NIKKI MACMILLAN

Bare Bulb Coffee
Kathleen, Georgia

Coffee Shops

Churches know coffee. Pastors are offered coffee when they stop by for a visit. Parishioners set coffee dates to discuss curriculums and plan events. We have weekly post-worship parties where the mud is served up in small paper cups. So, when the church thinks about its best bet for a business venture, coffee is a natural fit. Katie Rengers, pastor and leader of The Abbey in Birmingham, says of her coffee shop ministry, "We have coffee hour, but all the time."[2] To make good coffee is one thing, but to be church "all the time" is a significant enterprise, and one that the context increasingly demands.

Church guru Lovette Weems offers the church a distressing reality in this regard. In his 2010 *Christian Century* article called "No Shows," Weems confronts the staggering drop in mainline church attendance from 2001 to 2010. In that timespan, Episcopal, ELCA, and PCUSA churches all dropped in attendance by 15 percent or more and United Methodists

2. Katie Rengers, interview with author, May 21, 2015.

weren't far behind with a dip of 10 percent. Weems says that, while an aging constituency is a factor, "the most commonly accepted reason is that worshipers attend less frequently than before."[3] Katie, who serves at a large Episcopal church as part of her call, surmises that might be because mainline churches pig-pile their programming on Sunday and Wednesday nights and "reserving those times as sacred is just not happening anymore."

Nikki MacMillan, initiator of Bare Bulb Coffee in Kathleen, Georgia, echoes Katie's sentiment. She recalls her previous work at a local church and says, "We were doing great things, but nobody would come."[4] Most pastors and church leaders can relate to this dilemma and are accustomed to a cycle of head-hanging and trying harder. In that, Weems advises, "how people relate to church and their spiritual lives is changing. Churches may need to exercise new muscles to engage people in a greater variety of ways."[5] He then points to the book *Digital Cathedral* where author Keith Anderson establishes a three-fold task of the church, not to shoehorn their ministry into one or two time slots, but to continually "connect, convene, and converse."[6]

Further, Anderson says that "ministry is moving—and must move—from behind the closed doors of our church buildings into local and digital gathering places where people already gather, make meaning, and live out their faith in daily life."[7] Agreeing with Anderson as he includes the coffee shop as one of these places, Katie envisions The Abbey as "God's living room" and Nikki confirms, "Bare Bulb is a place where the community meets and gathers." Then she clarifies, "For the most part, we get to witness it—more than orchestrate it, we get to host it."

Churches that are accustomed to a pre-entitled place in the lives of its members might find it difficult to let go of the need to orchestrate, but Katie and Nikki offer a pattern for churches interested in becoming hosts.

Six Rules for Being a Good Host

1. *Mind the money.* Both The Abbey and Bare Bulb were born through a rigorous process of grant writing and other fundraising. Denominational and church support is available, but it requires a deeply

3. Weems, "No Shows."
4. Nikki MacMillan, interview with author, June 16, 2015.
5. Weems, "Fostering Conversations that Connect."
6. Ibid.
7. Anderson, "Mapping the 21st-Century Ministry Landscape."

thoughtful business plan. That is just the beginning. Launching a business and launching a church are uphill efforts on their own, doing both together is exceptionally tricky. Of utmost importance is for the church to recognize that, while the business opens the space for the church, it is not going to be its funding vessel. Nikki is direct about Bare Bulb, "the coffee shop is managing itself, the paying of the pastor to be the ministry person is taking outside help."

2. *Err on the side of extra.* In an age of perceived scarcity, Katie says, "good church is not fast, cheap, or easy" and points to the importance of having enough room so that it feels like "common, comfortable space." Likewise, Bare Bulb is double the size of a typical Starbucks so that they can foster the connecting, convening, and conversing that Anderson prescribes. They are being creative with space rentals and fundraising events as a way to help subsidize the cost of the extra space, something space-saving franchise shops don't have to do.

3. *Make it a potluck.* Not literally, of course, but churches understand the beauty of a potluck. It is the meal when everyone brings their best stuff for the good of the supper. Linda brings her bean dip, Christine brings a bottle of wine, and Ian grills the chicken. No one person is expected to manage it all. So it goes for the coffee shop. Both Katie and Nikki have baristas and business managers on staff, bringing their best stuff to the table. An experiment like this, void of people experienced in a coffee or food service setting, is doomed to fail.

4. *Ambience matters.* Like it or not, people are increasingly cautious of the church. If they dare walk into a church shop for coffee, they no doubt wonder what amount of proselytizing might come with it. On this account, it is important to be intentional about what the atmosphere communicates. Katie describes an evangelical-run coffee shop across town, "You would never know, going into their coffee shop, that they are Christian. To me, that's creepier than saying, 'Hey, we're Episcopal, take it or leave it.'"

5. *Allow for mingling.* While the coffee shops attract the common coffee consumer, they also serve as places where church folks can come hang out, drink coffee, host Bible studies, and meet friends. Both Nikki and Katie are using their denominational networks to drum up business. The natural temptation is to leverage this intersection of churched and unchurched communities to manufacture new conversations. "I've

had people come in and push a lot of theology," Nikki says, "but what I get to see, is that you don't have to do that. The Spirit does that."

6. *Send them away happy.* For most businesses, a happy customer is one that has enjoyed the product and will come back for another visit. The Abbey and Bare Bulb seek something with more depth and meaning than that. For that reason, both have established a regular Sunday afternoon worship service that includes liturgy and conversation. Katie remembers that the Abbey's service began organically, "At first, we didn't think we would have worship here every Sunday. Then we brought in the bishop to bless the empty space and a family came to me afterward and said, 'OK, we're ready, when do we start?'"

That question of "when?" is one of the most pressing for today's church. What time works best for worship? How do we squeeze in Sunday School? When does youth group start? Coffee shops, and enterprises of this ilk, provide the church an opportunity to offer something more than the typical answer, "See you Sunday! All are welcome!"; but to say "All are welcome, all the time."

MATT OVERTON

Mow Town
Vancouver, WA

Youth Ministry as Business

"We've created this 'ship in a bottle' experiment with our kids," Matt Overton says of contemporary youth ministry. "It looks nice in there but it never goes anywhere. The worst is when they walk out of youth group and realize this 'ship in a bottle' is never going to sail on the actual ocean."[8] The ship is carefully crafted with pizza, movies, games, and fellowship. It is fragile and easily disrupted if shaken by an irritable parent, self-entitled teenager, or board member that thinks they know better. It is never created from scratch, but always assembled with another boat in mind. Usually one that floated a long time ago. Then, as if toothpicks and balsa could stand the rigor of the sea, this is what the church sets before its young people to prepare them for the punishing severity of an adult life of faith. With all that it

8. Matt Overton, interview with author, July 1, 2015.

has to set them cruising in faith and rig them for living, it offers its youth a hobby. As if that is all they could possibly handle.

It is not just the youth being short-changed in this version of youth ministry. Lay and ordained leaders alike bear the weight of great frustration at the lack of commitment from youth and parents as they pour heart and soul into a program they believe in. Overton speaks for all of them. "I have always had the sense that I was doing a great job at something that only worked okay." Still, youth workers keep at it, nourished by the annual mission trip mountain top or the occasional turning point they witness in an adolescent. But nine years into his ordained ministry, even that was not enough to keep Matt going and so he changed gears and Mow Town was born.

The idea came to him as a result of his own home remodel. Through it, several of the youth group kids gave him a hand and he was grateful—not only for the work—but for the chance to join with them in a new kind of relationship. In working together, as it can often be on mission trips, hierarchical expectations were lifted and, with them, went obstructions to authentic knowing. He was especially pleased to see "kids that were on the fringes, those I might not see as frequently as I'd like at youth group," blossoming under the structure of work. From there, Matt set about creating a conversation with everyone from his church session, to social entrepreneurs, to prominent youth ministry voices Kenda Dean and Mark Devries, to consider the value of starting a faith-shaped business as a response to the shifts in family norms and adolescent culture. Wherever he went, he found heads nodding in support.

At first, Matt thought that the business would mimic his experience with youth on home remodeling, but labor laws turned him away from that. At some point, he would like to include IT support as a wing of the operation, but, for now, Mow Town is finding a niche as a light landscaping business. Matt, as the sole proprietor, takes calls, provides estimates, and assigns work. He has adult crew leaders that supervise the youth while on the job. Matt equips the leaders with what he calls "windshield questions" and encourages them to engage in intentional conversation about life and faith on the crew. The young people do everything from weeding, seeding, raking, hedging, to, of course, mowing. At the end of the day, they are paid a fair wage for what they do.

Andrew Root, author of Revisiting Relational Youth Ministry, points to the theological beauty of work like Overton's. "Youth ministry," he writes, "like all other ministry, is persons meeting persons in relationships bound by responsibility, for it is here that we meet Jesus as other."[9] Still, Matt has experienced push-back from those that suggest Mow Town is a way of brib-ing young people to be part of his program. To that he responds, "We are already in the bribery game, in a benign way, with snacks and couches. I'd rather bribe them with work. Then, if the young people reject Jesus, at least I can say I've provided them with some life skills." Further, in marrying faith with their job, this enterprise is helping to give the spiritual a position in the workplace, where most of the hours of their lives will be spent.

Beyond the possibility of a successful business, teaching of life skills, and formational infusing of faith and work, there just might be the growth of a new kind of success in youth ministry programming. Matt says, "part of the reason I'm losing kids on Sunday night is because I'm losing out to ballet classes or club soccer that costs $3,000. At least, in this, they have skin in the game." He recognizes that landscaping is not for every young person and is dedicated to expanding the business to include other kinds of work opportunities, but for now he is satisfied to see a growing buzz among the youth who see a vision and purpose to the program.

"We have a chance to re-shape American youth ministry," Matt asserts. The leaders of the reshaping will put down the balsa wood and tweezers of yesterday to pick up new tools for today. For Matt that means mowers, weed-wackers, mentors, "windshield questions," and a paycheck. Through these tools, we might give our youth not "influence but transcendence,"[10] not dodgeball and ice-cream but life-skills and a sense of worth, not a list-less hobby but a devotional job.

JESSICA WINDERWEEDLE

The Feed Truck
Kingston, New Jersey

Business among the People

If you want to volunteer with The Feed Truck in Kingston, New Jersey, you will be told that there are two rules. First, never let the coffee run out or go cold. Second, be good to people. If you can promise to "Keep Your Sunny Side Up," Jessica Winderweedle, Kingston Methodist pastor and food truck entrepreneur, will be happy to hand you a bright yellow T-shirt, offer all the

9. Root, *Revisiting Relational Youth Ministry*, 141.
10. Ibid., 140.

food you can eat, and put you to work. You will spend your time dishing up great tasting, healthy fare made with local ingredients and rubbing elbows with people from the neighborhood. "We work people really hard," Jessica says, "but they keep coming back. I think they enjoy being out among their neighbors. I love to help create that. This is an experiment of the church being outside of its four walls and trying to pleasantly surprise people every chance we get."[11]

Food trucks are known for their surprises, but not for pleasant ones. They are home to stale bread, soupy meat, and weak coffee. They go by cringe worthy names like barf buggy and roach coach. The online Urban Dictionary, always good for offering an unfiltered commentary, draws the image of "a catering truck, especially one which frequents blue collar places of work; generally, a modded pickup truck with insulated diamond-pattern doors covering a refrigerator case and a warmer unit with attached griddle."

Contemporary food truck culture is reshaping the assumptions to a degree, with even *The Boston Globe* pronouncing that "mobile eateries once dubbed 'roach coaches' have evolved into haute cuisine."[12] Still, to make it in the food truck world, every aspect of the business must surpass expectations, especially if it is located in a high-brow place near Princeton, New Jersey.

For The Feed Truck, this started by generating the grant funding and relational partnerships to procure a beautiful, state of the art truck. "We were fortunate," Jessica says, "to find a Methodist guy in Rochester, New York, who is a food truck fabricator. Through the grapevine this guy found out what we wanted to do and he was excited about combining his skill set with ministry. He did a beautiful custom build, pretty much at cost." From there, Jessica, who has a background in the food service world, designed a menu that could be fixed with products from New Jersey farms. Finally, the ministry began the work of establishing rapport with local entities to promote what they were doing and park for business hours. Now The Feed Truck has a standing invitation to set up near Princeton Seminary housing, takes regular calls to show up at church events, and has a weekly gig at the Farmer's Market. As Jessica puts it, "We are definitely in the mode of dancing with whomever asks us." Still, while all of this is good for keeping the business going, it was not their original intention in starting the ministry enterprise.

11. Jessica Winderweedle, interview with author, June 17, 2015.

12. Abutaleb, "Food Trucks Fueled by Fusion," *The Boston Globe*.

"We really wanted to get on college campuses," Jessica says. "That is still our ultimate goal, to spend as much time on college campuses as we can and we are trying to work every angle as we can." While evangelical campus groups like Campus Crusade and Intervarsity Christian Fellowship continue to fill campus chapels,[13] college ministry remains a mystery to the mainline church, which sees few options outside of the mimicry of pop-Christian crazes. The Feed Truck is committed to being something different though. "It's not about being cool or hooking people in with some trend," Jessica says, "but about being able to engage the community in deeper conversations."

One of the deeper conversations The Feed Truck hopes to cultivate is, quite appropriately, centered around food. Increasingly, words like "organic," "gluten," "GMO," and "paleo" are rolling off the tongue; they can be heard on campus, certainly, but elsewhere as well. Credit Michael Pollan, author of *The Omnivore's Dilemma*, for breaking the ground for new discussion around holistically rewarding eating habits. He suggests that "the way we eat represents our most profound engagement with the natural world. Daily, our eating turns nature into culture, transforming the body of the world into our bodies and minds."[14] For The Feed Truck, this means stirring community well-being and agricultural sustainability into the too-often-rote act of eating. They support local suppliers, highlight the work of non-profits around food-based issues, and help organizations that are working to alleviate food insecurity. Not only are these concerns in vogue for the present day, they are natural for a tradition that has been reciting a prayer about "daily bread" for the last two thousand years.

While The Feed Truck caters discussion and great eats, it's also serving what Jessica calls "intangible good" to the community. She explains, "I can't always put my finger on what the ministry is or does; there is no bullet-point list. But there's not a week that goes by where I don't hear someone say, 'Oh this is a church thing?' Then they act surprised because nothing about it felt obnoxious or offensive." Amidst the current church climate, this is a great compliment and no easy task. Indeed, not every church can start a food truck business or gain access to a slew of young adults, but most can take a step or two in the long road to recovering reputation. If nothing else, the church can start by following two rules: never let the coffee run out and be good to people.

13. Intervarsity Christian Fellowship, "Intervarsity Sees Growth Despite Challenge."
14. Pollan, *The Omnivore's Dilemma*, 10.

BRINGING IT HOME

Jesus said, "I came that you might have life and have it abundantly."

He does life like nobody does life, just ask the empty tomb.

From the very beginning to this very day, being a Christian means being in the uniquely abundant business of life.

Like with every good farmer, being in the business of life means caring about things that maybe you didn't care about before. Like flowers and rain and the moon and the dirt and the good will of every human being. Even those human beings that hold up regular business.

Curious things happen at the church during the work week.

Like running into disheveled young women standing at water fountains in an otherwise empty building. We can pass her by because she is not on the agenda and someone else will take care of her. But, if we listen to the business ministry taking place through The Abbey, Bare Bulb, Mow Town, and The Feed Truck, we will hear a call to be on the job. We will sense a tug to allow her needs, not our schedule, to dictate the terms of our interaction. This is the real shift that these profiles of enterprise mean to model.

If we are in the business of life, we will discover that her fiancé committed suicide this week, that the funeral was yesterday, and that she slept in her car in the church parking lot and now her car battery is dead.

If we are in the business of life, we will listen to her and learn that she doesn't go to church, but she did come here for Alcoholics Anonymous once, so this is where she came after the funeral.

If we are in the business of life, we will not be overly concerned with how inadequate we are or how we really should get her off church property or how efficiently we can pass her along so that we can go back to the business of being the church.

If we are in the business of life, we will care about this stranger, this person, this human being and what she's going through.

That's how it is in this new way of ministry as business where we offer "God's living room," hold "windshield" conversations, and "keep our sunny side up." There's no way of telling if this enterprise will ever turn a profit, but if we are in the business of life we won't care about profit like we used to. We will care about something else. Maybe we will even care about things that we didn't care so much about before, like flowers and rain and the moon and the dirt and the good will of every human being.

CHAPTER 10

Tiny Wild Strawberries

Cooperative Parishes

Finally, we are back to where we started from in the first place. We are in the hills of western Maine, where Mission at the Eastward still plugs along with steady, albeit quieting, resiliency. The same sturdy people try to guide the same rickety undertakings in an attempt to outlast the closing of anything for good.

We are standing outside of my home church, the one that owned the old green manse that was my home until the seventh grade. There is a sign in front of the church that plainly says, "West Mills Community Church," if you can read through peeling paint. The doors and windows are locked and maybe rusted in place. Rumor has it that the drainage system was installed all wrong when they rebuilt the place after a fire in 1977, that's why the mold is so bad and that's why it is shuttered. God only knows how long it has been since someone was inside the building.

Not so long ago, it was home to sparsely attended Sunday morning services, Vacation Bible School for the community, volleyball teams that played in its makeshift sand court, and, most notably, a widely popular youth drama troupe and choir, "The Eastward Players" and the "Sparrow's Song Youth Choir." Whatever pride a one-road town can have in itself, this community had for the drama troupe and choir. It was a place where teenagers found an outlet for their talents as they travelled all over the eastern seaboard with their act, but the best performances were the ones held in this square building, because here the audience beamed for them. Today, though, there is no worship service, no VBS, no volleyball, and, perhaps most sadly, no "Players" or "Sparrows."

"I wonder if we could get this place going again," we say out loud.

We are there with a group of church people from Delaware who have traveled to Maine on a mission trip. Kristen, a seventeen-year old from the church group, is there with us.

"Why can't we?" she asks.

She startles us with her question.

What does she know? She is exceptionally good-hearted, but she is just a teenager from a church that sits over nine hours away. Hers is a church with three hundred years of history, pristine carpets and pews, and a million-dollar annual operating budget. She never got a sticker for Sunday school attendance here or colored on the warped wooden pews during the sermon. I know she never went to one of the community dances in the basement, the ones where Barbara watched with her binoculars from across the street, just certain we were all going to hell. For sure she has never walked the back field in July and picked the tiny wild strawberries one at a time. Yes, I am now her pastor and I have brought her here from far away, but what does she know about this place—this place of the most beautiful dirt, roots, and weeds?

"I don't know," we tell her, "maybe we can."

How many of today's mainline churches face a fate like that of the West Mills Community Church? The landscape of our communities have changed and our churches, so often designed by those that figured they would be needed there forever, lack the flexibility that fledgling, mostly evangelical, startups have. And it is not just that, as if that is not painful enough, while they are shrinking and watching the "fun" churches bloat, they are coming face to face with their reliance on another's goodwill to maintain any shape at all.

It is in this reality of reliance that the old model of a cooperative parish, one that Mission at the Eastward has modeled so well, might just need to reemerge. Through it, we can admit that there is an odd hypnotism to pastoral models that bind us from exploring what best fits a congregation and the surrounding community. We can set aside a blind acceptance of "One Church-One Pastor" as the best arrangement for every worshipping community.

To get there though, we must first acknowledge the anxiety that comes with letting go of what once was or what we hoped would be in order to shift directions and do something else. Many church members can name and, often hauntingly, describe a pastor they loved. This pastor was one that preached great sermons, filled the pews, expanded the building, had great teeth, and visited every member. To consider a cooperative model, even when faced with no other feasible financial option, is to achingly let go of the dream of ever having another one of "him" again. It is a burial, of sorts. Still, it can be encouraging to know that some churches are finding unexpected and life-giving side-effects. And so, we close our storytelling with three inspiring narratives of churches in partnership.

ANDY EVENSON & BOB IERIEN

Lebanon Lutheran Cooperative Ministry
Lebanon, PA

Starting a Cooperative Parish

Over and above all other things, you can count on the church for showing the world how to split up. Since the beginning, it has modeled a mastery of divorce, for that there is no denial. Congratulations, church. A few of its ruptures are well-known by a place, like Chalcedon, where, in the fifth century, a council created language for the nature of Jesus and the Coptics broke away. Some are notorious by their theological arguments, like the Trinity-based "filioque," which drummed out the East–West schism in the eleventh century. Others, like "The Reformation," which plucked the Protestants from the Catholics in the sixteenth century,[1] are best remembered by household names like Luther and Calvin. Local churches, who lack access to such great platforms, have to make due with smaller issues in their attempts to mimic the "take my ball and go home" strategies of its ancestry. In the case of two small churches in Lebanon, Pennsylvania, the split of 1844 came on account of language.

Pastor Andy Evenson, one of the two founding pastors of the Lebanon Lutheran Cooperative Ministry (LLCM), remembers moving to the area, "I saw that my congregation was a half a block away from another ELCA congregation and I realized this is kind of silly."[2] He did some research and, it turned out, that in 1844, one faction of the Lutheran congregation wanted

1. Tickle, *The Great Emergence*, 4.
2. Andy Evenson, interview with author, June 12, 2015.

to keep worshipping in German and another wanted to speak English. Unable to reconcile differences, one broke off from the other and started another church within spitting distance. It wasn't long, less than a decade even, before both churches were worshipping in English, but the divisive damage was already done. Today these two churches are joined with two others by the LLCM, but the larger church would do well to remember that this divorce, one that took five minutes (relatively) to enact, took over a hundred and fifty years to amend.

According to Pastor Bob Ierien, another LLCM founding pastor, the Synod deserves credit for launching the conversation and setting the tone for the cooperative parish. "They cultivated a series of conversations facilitated by the synod director of evangelical mission," he says. "We talked about various models for shared ministry." They considered the two-point parish, multi-site congregations, and churches joined in an area mission strategy. As the four churches emerged with a willingness to join in the cooperative relationship, the synod offered a template for official agreement that ordained and lay leaders worked to adapt for their purposes.

The pastors managed the division of pastoral labor by playing to their strengths with program and setting up a rotating schedule of worship leadership which allows both to lead at all the churches. They sketched out a schedule for how they would tackle location equality for major events and high holidays. Of all the issues hashed out in their negotiations, Bob notes that, predictably, the most "ticklish" was that of money. Ultimately, the association landed on a proportional funding model broken into three components.[3]

1. Called staff: Each congregation contributes a proportional share based on worship attendance.

2. Visitation pastor: This share is based on percentage of visits done to the congregation by the visitation of the pastor. This is important because, as Bob points out, "one of our congregations has two home-bound members, another has over half of the visits."

3. Office and ministry expenses (VBS, confirmation, youth, etc.): All four churches pay the same amount. Since all have the opportunity to benefit equally, these are divided equally.

---

3. Bob Ierien, interview with author, June 9, 2015.

Cooperative parishes are often seen as a money saving measure for dwindling churches, but Andy and Bob point to the funding model to show why that is not always the case. "It's not the cheapest way forward for these congregations," Andy says. "I think a lot of these kinds of churches could have a quarter-time pastor and not do much more than meet on a Sunday and get by real cheap for a long time—but that's not what we're doing."

Instead, they are doing real things. They are hosting Vacation Bible School programs, running confirmation classes, launching neighborhood events, and planting a community garden. Through the LLCM, these small churches take part in a rotating homeless shelter ministry, share a pub and theology discussion group, and go on a mission trip. Most small churches assume that these kinds of ministries are not for them because they lack the critical mass. What fun is a youth group with only two teenagers? How can we staff a church dinner with so few volunteers? Andy says it well, "as churches get smaller the pastor kind of ends up as a chaplain, now we basically function as a large church in multiple locations."

It is from this posture of togetherness that these four churches are finding a sense of renewed life. There is something new to mention during the announcements, a sense of pride in their online presence, and each of the congregations has enjoyed new members joining their body. In introducing Gilson Waldkoenig and William Avery's book, *Cooperating Congregations*, James Lewis presciently describes LLCM as he suggests that

> successful cooperative parishes are driven more by a passion for Christian mission than by a struggle for survival. It is this passion for mission that fuels their creativity and enables them to adapt in imaginative ways to settings that are basically hostile to traditional congregational life. Congregations in such demanding settings are most likely to thrive when they move beyond a concern for survival and toward a commitment to mission.[4]

The cooperative work being done by Bob, Andy, and the churches in the LLCM is an uphill climb. It is work that runs counter to the somewhat recent paradigm that dishonestly claims, "a church is only a church if they have a building and pay a pastor to work full time." Without these, it is presumed, the church has failed. What LLCM is finding in sharing their ministry leaders and locations, is something quite opposite of failure. Their Synod is excited, their pastors are motivated, and their people are engaging the gospel in new ways. Besides, even if none of that were true, these

---

4. Waldkoenig and Avery, *Cooperating Congregations*, 5.

churches are making a new name for themselves—and maybe setting a new pattern for the rest of us. Instead of being known for how they are split up, they are charting a course for how to get back together.

MELISSA RUDOLPH

North Carroll Cooperative Parish
Upperco & Hampstead, Maryland

When a Cooperative Parish Cooperates

Maybe it's time to start burying small, rural churches. The studies[5] prove what we know in our gut, these churches are dying off with a disease for which there is no cure. Carol Howard Merritt offers the diagnosis, "we're seeing devastating effects of being a largely rural, white, older church. As agriculture changes, areas where there were 5,000 farmers and a community of banks, post offices, hardware stores, and schools supporting them have now been reduced to five agro-businesses. The bank, post office, stores, and schools are closing and younger generations need to migrate to urban areas for employment."[6] We cannot possibly expect these churches to stay open when every other institutional structure is shuttering the windows. That is to say, we cannot expect them to stay open *in the same way*.

Instead of closing, some are doing an internal inventory. They are positioning themselves to admit that, as their towns and memberships shrink, so does their influence. They are approaching their future with humility, realizing that they cannot go it alone and still do the kind of ministry that they want to do. Rev. Melissa Rudolph describes how, in 2011, the three churches she serves were "struggling in different ways. Two of them were experiencing major declines in attendance and could not support a full time pastor."[7] For them, the answer was to form the North Carroll Cooperative Parish, a United Methodist Community.

To join the parish meant giving up some of their autonomy and developing a steering committee to develop a funding model and implement cooperative strategy, but it paid off almost immediately. According to Melissa, "the initial enthusiasm meant the churches were actually cooperating more

5. "National Congregations Study," Duke University, 2012.
6. Blum, "Merritt of the Mainline," *Religion in American History*.
7. Melissa Rudolph, interview with author, June 15, 2015.

quickly than we anticipated at first. The reality is that many parishioners are friends, coworkers, and neighbors who already had relationships but attended separate churches." Not only that, one of the churches has doubled its worship attendance (from fifty to over one hundred) in the four years of the cooperative's life.

Melissa believes that much of the NCCP success comes from a new disposition in the lay leadership. "It's less about survival, and more about thanksgiving." This supports what Gilson Waldkoenig and William Avery contend. "By forming a cooperative, congregations consistently change from turning in upon themselves to adapting a mission stance of service beyond the walls of their churches. Preoccupation with survival is wide-spread in small membership congregations. But cooperatives have led many small congregations into a mission posture."[8]

There are a variety of features that give NCCP a mission posture and make them, as Melissa puts it, "a cooperative that actually cooperates." First, they share the pastors. Melissa and her husband, John, serve as co-pastors of the parish and have developed a rotating schedule for worship leadership that regularly puts them in each of the churches on Sunday mornings. Second, they worship together. Anytime there is a fifth Sunday in a month, they have one combined service and alternate where that is. Melissa notes that, "for some people they have lived in the same town their whole lives and had never gone to one of these other churches." Third, they do things together. They share church dinners and service projects, but, beyond that, they have devised a visitation ministry that joins the congregations in caring for one another's hospitalized and homebound members. This is of utmost importance because, Melissa says, "the biggest challenge we are having is the growth. We need help just to keep up with the pastoral need."

Not every cooperative parish will replicate this kind of success. The groundwork for NCCP was laid with the support and encouragement of the denomination. That groundwork was paired with dynamic pastors who share the pastoral sense to continually acknowledge, as Melissa does, "that these people, they built the church. Their grandparents laid the cornerstone."

Then, alongside the support of the denomination and skill of the pastors, NCCP has an invested and creative community of lay leaders. There are members, like Jane, who started a bring-a-visitor contest. She split the congregation into teams and gave them pom-poms and cheers. Some might call such a scheme hokey or trite, but their church is calling it fruitful. That

8. Waldkoenig and Avery, *Cooperating Congregations*, 5.

congregation is seeing new people of all ages joining their rolls. It is as if these churches have heard Carol Howard Merritt's warning, "it is easy for our churches and denominations to slip into a narrative of decline which leads us to impart a message of deprivation: come to our church because we need more hope, money, and energy (which doesn't sound like good news at all)."[9] Instead of deprivation, theirs is now a message of cooperation and generosity—even to the grave.

Melissa illustrates this with poignancy, "We wanted to start this football league, but the only flat ground we had in the parish was a portion of the Greenmount Cemetery that has not been populated yet." Because it would, one day, be home to burials, they assumed it would be off limits. But one of the members whose plot is in that ground spoke up for the league. She said, "Even when I go, they can play right on top of me. I would just love to know that these kids are playing there." What that member understands is that burial, for us and for our churches, is an inevitable reality. It will come for us one day, and, when it does, there will still be a place for life and abundance in the midst of it. In fact, if part of what NCCP is doing is burying the old way of being a small church, perhaps it is time to ready the shovels and start to dig.

STEVE ROW AND JONI JAMES

Mission at the Eastward
Hills of Western Maine

Cooperating outside of Geographical Bounds

When Bill Burger first cast the vision for Camp at the Eastward in the 1950s, it was meant to be the pride and joy of the small congregations of the Mission at the Eastward (MATE) cooperative parish. Like the Lemon Stream that creates its boundary, the camp was supposed to shimmer with light and make room for life in the hard nature of Maine. It was to be where the children of these churches, many from difficult homes, would grow together and experience the beauty of Christian friendship. In the beginning, the campers slept in tents and ate meals under a lean-to. But, over time, a total of eight simple cabins, a crafts building, a recreation hall, and a bath

---

9. Howard-Merritt, *Reframing Hope*, 78.

house were constructed, along with a log-cabin dining hall built from trees harvested off the property.

Generations of campers slept under the branches of the tall Hemlock trees in Starks, Maine. Today, parents and grandparents look forward to registering their kids to attend their childhood camp, maybe even sleep in the same cabin they did as a child. They will walk the forest trail and set up their bunk for them. They will stop by the outdoor chapel with the wooden benches. They will go to the arts and crafts building and show them where their name is painted on a popsicle stick and tacked to the rafters. It is still there from thirty years ago. They will, for just a moment, glow.

A week, or even a summer day, at the camp quickly reveals that ribbons of Burger's original vision shimmer through the place even now. Chores are shared, races are run, songs are passed down, and the campfire rages on. There is a special beauty about life together there and it is experienced by the elementary school kids and senior highs alike. And yet, undeniably, the camp illustrates so much of what is difficult about this season of life in the cooperative parish. Common at the camp, and throughout MATE, are words like "deferred maintenance," "shortfall," "understaffed," and "empty." Joni James, a former camper and longtime camp director laments, "For years we've 'made do' and tightened the purse strings and it shows—both to the campers and to the parents. Camp is actually a symptom of the larger issue within MATE; lack of involvement, lack of funds, and painfully, a lack of young people."[10]

Like the camp, many of the original pieces of Mission at the Eastward remain in place, but precariously so. The small churches plug on, more or less, but their experience of cooperation has faded, mostly from long-held grudges that nobody can remember starting. The housing ministry still brings groups from New Jersey, Pennsylvania, and Delaware to contribute to low-income housing needs, but fewer participants make the trip. The MATE staff and lay council remain dedicated, but makeshift and always revolving. All of it is fragile and could die. Some would say that it should. But, chances are, it won't.

MATE began as an innovation of the small church model. Its roots are in adaptive resiliency. Nancy Ammerman opines, "that some congregations find ways to adapt in the face of such shifts in their environment is far more remarkable than that some congregations die."[11] MATE has always

---

10. Joni James, interview with author, August 11, 2015.

11. Ammerman, *Congregations and Community*, 347.

typified that. So instead of lamenting what was lost, remarkable MATE enters another season of change, not just for survival, but from a sense of stewardship for what has been before—for all of the names on all of those rafters in all of its ministries. For that, MATE is listening to Ammerman as she goes on, "congregations do not adapt on their own" and further notes the importance of other structures in helping to develop a creative conversation.[12] MATE is finding those conversation partners, quite organically, through the church relationships formed by their years of involvement in the housing ministry.

Current Mission at the Eastward coordinator, Rev. Steve Row, dreams, "I see MATE expanding its horizons to include the churches and other organizations that come to Maine to volunteer their more-than-ample energy and resources to our mutual ministries. I would like to see some of those churches more involved in the programming and decision-making processes."[13] Sharing leadership with "out of staters" is no short order for the hearty and independent-minded New Englanders of Mission at the Eastward. But these are not ordinary outsiders, several of the groups that Steve refers to have been traveling to Maine in mission for over twenty years. Further, he suggests that MATE make mission more of "a two-way street: In other words, MATE could offer to send groups from Maine to assist in ministries to more urban areas just as groups have come to Maine for the past several decades." There is a level of trust built between these churches already, trust that might lead to a new way of being a cooperative parish in spite of geographical limitations.

According to Joni, the shift to being a new kind of cooperative parish—one that dismisses distance as an obstacle—is already benefiting Camp at the Eastward. She reports that relationships with churches from out of state have brought fresh faces with lots of campers, staff, and work groups. She attributes this new blood as the inspiration for home-grown improvement projects, as well as refreshed involvement of old camp friends. Steve Row turns to history to explain the change, "MATE's mission statement highlights the saying of one of its founders, 'Reach the last house on the last road.' What I think we are discovering is that that road extends a lot longer than any of us expected, way beyond central Maine to Massachusetts, New Jersey, Pennsylvania, Delaware and beyond."

12. Ibid., 344.
13. Stephen Row, e-mail message to author, August 19, 2015.

BRINGING IT HOME

We ultimately did what good-hearted Kristen thought we could.

After several years of sending massive work teams, we got the place going again.

But it was an altogether different place.

After a season of thoughtful planning, the local stakeholders agreed that this new place should set its feet in its tradition of hosting the East-ward Players. So, when it reopened, it did so as a community theater. Diane Leeman, the inventive dean of the playhouse, says, "Even though it's not a church anymore, we continue to think of what we do here as a ministry. It's a way of people being able to experience a creative process that they might not otherwise experience."[14]

Before, there was a pulpit and cross. Now there are stage lights and a box set.

The basement, which once held church suppers, serves as a changing room and a prop closet.

It was painted off-white before. It is bright yellow now, except for one side where an enormous mural of creation was painted by locals and church volunteers. You can't miss it.

It was closed before. Yes, because of the mold. But even before that, even at its best, it welcomed a dozen worshippers for an hour on Sunday mornings. So it was always mostly closed. Now it bustles with people on all days at all hours. Some are there to paint sets. Others to rehearse. Six weekends a year the community crowds in to see their family and friends in a show.

Once it was called West Mills Community Church and it belonged to the denomination. Now it's called the Sparrow's Nest and it's loved by the community. Not only that, it has created a cooperative community, one that spans the coastline from Maine to Delaware.

Still, you know, even when you do something else, some things remain the same. Trouble still comes. Small town politics and gossip still manage to creep into its work. The hearty production team worries if they will have enough to give it a go next season. The snowy weather functions like a dictator. But the building gives all it has, the people are warm, the clock moves as a clock should move, and, when the summer comes, the tiny wild

14. Ohm, "Sparrow's Nest Arts Center in Industry Takes Center Stage."

strawberries still grow. Go sometime and taste them for yourself. I wonder if you will ever taste a strawberry like the ones that grow in that place. That beautiful place.[15]

15. Visit www.missionattheeastward.org or www.ephm.org to investigate a mission trip of your own.

Bibliography

Abutaleb, Yasmeen. "Food Trucks Fueled by Fusion." *The Boston Globe*, August 17, 2014. Accessed August 19, 2015. https://www.bostonglobe.com/metro/2014/08/16/food-truck-study-shows-roach-coaches-yore-have-given-way-fusion-cuisine-that-bridges-gaps/u6aUa7R8wvuKW7YZ1bItuM/story.html.

Ammerman, Nancy. *Congregations and Community*. New Brunswick, NJ: Rutgers University, 1997.

Anderson, Keith. "Mapping the 21st Century Ministry Landscape." *The BTS Center*, September 26, 2014. Accessed August 19, 2015. http://www.thebtscenter.org/mapping-the-21st-century-ministry-landscape/.

Austin, Daniel. "Farmington Voters Give Ok to Road Building Funds." *Lewiston Daily Sun*, June 16, 1988.

Banks, Adelle M. "Women Take the Reins at Three Tall-Steeple Mainline Churches." *The Christian Century*, September 2, 1014. Accessed August 19, 2015. http://www.christiancentury.org/article/2014-09/cracks-stained-glass-ceiling-women-reach-prominent-pulpits.

Barna Group. "Number of Female Senior Pastors in Protestant Churches Doubles in Past Decade." Last modified September 14, 2009. https://www.barna.org/barna-update/leadership/304-number-of-female-senior-pastors-in-protestant-churches-doubles-in-past-decade#.VdUwqmCzVFJ.

Barth, Karl. *Church Dogmatics*. Vol. 4, Parts 1–4: *The Doctrine of Reconciliation*. Edited by G. W. Bromiley and T. F. Torrance. Edinburgh: T. & T. Clark, 1956–69.

Bass, Dorothy C. *Practicing our Faith: A way of Life for a Searching People*. San Francisco: Jossey-Bass, 1997.

Black Methodists for Church Renewal. "Our History." Accessed August 19, 2015. http://www.bmcrumc.org/history.

Bloom, Linda, and Kathy L. Gilbert. "United Methodists Achieve Milestones Despite Differences." *United Methodist News*. Accessed August 19, 2015. http://www.umc.org/news-and-media/will-disputes-stymie-united-methodists-in-2016.

Blum, Edward. "Merritt of the Mainline." *Religion in America*. Last modified December 20, 2012. http://usreligion.blogspot.com/2012/12/merritt-of-mainline.html.

Bonhoeffer, Dietrich. *Discipleship*. Minneapolis: Fortress, 2001.

Bosch, David. *Transforming Mission: Paradigm Shifts in Theology of Mission*. Maryknoll, NY: Orbis, 1991.

Branson, Mark, and Nicholas Warnes, eds. *Starting Missional Churches: Life with God in the Neighborhood*. Downers Grove, IL: InterVarsity, 2014.

Buter-Bass, Diana. *Christianity After Religion: The End of the Church and the Birth of a New Spiritual Awakening*. New York: Harper Collins, 2013.

Carroll, Jackson. *God's Potters: Pastoral Leadership and the Shaping of Congregations*. Grand Rapids: Eerdmans, 2006.

———. *Mainline to the Future: Congregations for the 21st Century*. Louisville, KY: Westminster John Knox, 2000.

Carter, Joe. "How to Tell the Difference between PCA and PC(USA)." *The Gospel Coalition*, June 23, 2014. http://www.thegospelcoalition.org/article/how-to-tell-the-difference-between-the-pca-and-pcusa.

Cartwright, R. L. "Lumberjack Sky Pilots." *MNOPEDIA*. September 20, 2013. http://www.mnopedia.org/group/lumberjack-sky-pilots.

Cohen, Chaim. "Eden." In *The Oxford Dictionary of the Jewish Religion: Second Edition*, edited by Adele Berlin and Maxine Grossman, 229. New York: Oxford University, 2011.

Disney, Walt, et al. *Pinocchio*. Burbank, CA: Walt Disney Productions, 1940.

Dykstra, Craig, and James Hudnut-Beumler. "The National Organizational Structures of Protestant Denominations: An Invitation to a Conversation." In *The Organizational Revolution: Presbyterians and American Denominationalism*, edited by John M. Mulder, Milton J. Coalter, and Louis B. Weeks, 307–32. Louisville, KY: Westminster John Knox, 1992.

Faith Communities Today. 2010 *National Survey of Congregations*. Accessed August 19, 2015. http://faithcommunitiestoday.org/sites/faithcommunitiestoday.org/files/2010FrequenciesV1.pdf.

Geores, Carl. *The Journey of Faith: The Leeds, Wales, Hartford Parish, and the Mission at the Eastward*. 1952–1988. No loc: n.p., 1989.

Glick, Melissa. "Nave Gallery and Nave Annex: A Project of Love." *Boston Art Makers*. Accessed, August 19, 2015. http://bostonartmakers.org/2015/06/26/nave-gallery-and-nave-annex-a-project-of-love/.

Guder, Darrell L. "Practical Theology in the Service of the Missional Church." In *Theology in Service of the Church: Essays in Honor of Joseph D. Small 3RD*, edited by Charles A. Wiley et al., 13–22. Louisville: Geneva, 2008.

Howard-Merritt, Carol. *Reframing Hope: Vital Ministry in a New Generation*. Lanham, MD: Rowman and Littlefield, 2014.

Intervarsity Christian Fellowship. "Intervarsity Sees Growth Despite Challenge." Last modified April 25, 2010. http://www.intervarsity.org/news/intervarsity-sees-growth-despite-challenge.

Krejcir, R. J. "Statistics on Pastors." *Into Thy Word*. Accessed August 19, 2015. http://www.intothyword.org/apps/articles/default.asp?articleid=36562.

Lewis, C. S. *Mere Christianity*. New York: Macmillan, 1960.

National Congregations Study. 2012 *National Congregations Study*. Accessed August 19, 2015. http://www.soc.duke.edu/natcong/.

Ohm, Rachel. "Sparrow's Nest Arts Center in Industry Takes Center Stage." *Kennebec Journal*, July 13, 2013. Accessed August 19, 2015. http://www.centralmaine.com/2013/07/13/sparrows-nest-arts-center-in-industry-takes-center-stage/.

On Being, with Krista Tippett. "Transcript for Martin Marty—America's Changing Religious Landscape." Last modified November 2, 2006. http://www.onbeing.org/program/america039s-changing-religious-landscape-conversation-martin-marty/transcript/603.

Oxford Dictionaries, s.v. "Nave." Accessed August 19, 2015, http://www.oxforddictionaries. com/us/definition/american_english/nave.

Pope Francis. "Address of the Holy Father Pope Francis." Audience with Representatives of the Churches and Ecclesial Communities and of the Different Religions. Speech given at Clementine Hall, Vatican City, March 20, 2013.

PBS Frontline. "The Jesus Factor: An Interview with Richard Cizik." Last modified April 29, 2004. http://www.pbs.org/wgbh/pages/frontline/shows/jesus/interviews/cizik. html

Pollan, Michael. *The Omnivore's Dilemma: A Natural History of Four Meals.* New York: Penguin, 2006.

Quoist, Michel. *Prayers.* Franklin, WI: Sheed & Ward, 1954.

"Religion: Preacher in the Woods," *Time Magazine,* May 26, 1947. http://www.time.com/ time/magazine/article/0,9171,793749,00.html#ixzz1XHeFnR00.

Renfro, Blake. "The Reunification of American Methodism: 1916–1939." MA thesis, Louisiana State University, 2010.

Richter, Conrad. *A Simple Honorable Man.* New York: Knopf, 1962.

Root, Andrew. *Revisiting Relational Youth Ministry: From a Strategy of Influence to a Theology of Incarnation.* Downers Grove, IL: InterVarsity, 2007.

Seaton, Tony. "Huntington WV Riverfront Homeless Evicted from 'Tent City.'" YouTube video, posted by "NewsYouNeed," February 12, 2008, https://www.youtube.com/ watch?v=aRS_KEIM0EA.

Seow, C. L. *Homosexuality and the Christian Community.* Louisville, KY: Westminster John Knox, 1996.

Sherman, Rose. "The Myth That Nurses Leave Nursing." *The Emerging Leader.* Last modified November 11, 2013. http://www.emergingrnleader.com/the-myth-that-nurses-leave-nursing/.

Tickle, Phyllis. *The Great Emergence: How Christianity is Changing and Why.* Grand Rapids: Baker, 2008.

Tucker, Valerie. "Planting Farewell Planned." *The Irregular,* September 29, 2010.

Van Engen, Charles. *God's Missionary People: Rethinking the Purpose of the Local Church.* Grand Rapids: Baker, 1991.

Waldkoenig, Gilson, and William Avery. *Cooperating Congregations: Portraits of Mission Strategies.* Bethesda, MD: Alban Institute, 1999.

Weems, Lovette H. "No Shows." *The Christian Century,* September 22, 2010. Accessed August 19, 2015. http://www.christiancentury.org/article/2010-09/no-shows.

Weems, Lovette, H. "Fostering Conversations that Connect." *Leading Ideas,* August 5, 2015. Accessed August 19, 2015. http://www.churchleadership.com/leadingideas/ updates/150805.html.

Afterword

by C. Scott Planting

"Be a good pastor and follow your hearts delight."—CARL GEORES

At first light, *Sunbeam* nurse Sharon Daley and I leave the boat carrying L. L. Bean bags of breakfast sandwiches and thermoses of coffee. We walk down the old wooded wharf past centuries old fish houses to Harbor Point, also known as Probation Point, to the three story dormitory that captains built for their sternmen. Sternmen are the "migrant laborers" of the ocean, fishermen who work for a time on a boat then move on. The work is hard, the pay is good, and no one asks much about where you came from—hence the name "probation point." As sternmen make their way down to the docks, and row out to fishing boats, Sharon and I greet them with breakfast sandwiches and coffee. Fishermen take a sandwich, fill a mug of coffee, and nod "thanks." One young man lingers. "Where you from?" he asks. We tell him the *Sunbeam,* the 74-foot boat of the Maine Sea Coast Mission, which has provided health and spiritual care to Maine's outer islands for over a century. "Join us for dinner."

The *Sunbeam* is docked on Matinicus Island, 33 miles out to sea, the most remote inhabited island on the Atlantic seaboard. The *Sunbeam* visits the Matinicus in the winter and summer. In the winter, the island is home to forty souls. There are no year-round stores, or shops or places to eat, or doctors or policemen, and only one industry. It is where the fog drops around you like a curtain for days at a time and the ferry comes once a month (if you're lucky) in winter. As the natives are fond of saying: You live here because you love it, or you don't live here at all.

The young sternman who we met in the morning, hoodie up, boards the *Sunbeam* at close to nine that night. He needs help and asks to see Sharon and me. He tells us a story of abuse and addiction. "I'm lost," he says. "I need help; I need God. I want some peace in my life." I say a prayer and Sharon offers to set him up with a counselor at an addiction counseling center on the mainland. Then she warns him, "I know your captain. He's a good man, a fair man. But he won't tolerate bad behavior." He leaves the *Sunbeam*, spirits lifted. Aptly named, the boat is a place of peace and of healing. An island woman who has gone through much struggle in her life told me, "Every time I come on the *Sunbeam* I get a little piece of myself back."

Forty years ago, I sat in the corner of the cramped, book filled office of Carl Geores, the co-founder of Mission at the Eastward (MATE), described in the first chapter of this book. "What more do you want in life?" he asked me.

I was finishing a summer internship at MATE where I'd been the pastor of three small churches in the foothills of Western Maine. The parish covered 500 square miles. Three services every Sunday. One week I was a camp counselor at camp at the Eastward in Starks, Maine. It was truly a wilderness camp site and I found myself piled into a cabin with a dozen ten-year-old boys. Funerals. I remember calling Carl after I'd been asked to officiate at a service for a young man who'd died of ALS, Lou Gehrig's disease. Carl's response, find a *Book of Common Worship*. "You'll know what to do," he said.

Neighbors helped me plant a garden, others taught me to fly fish. One morning around 4:30, Carl called me on the phone, waking me up. "What are the people across the street doing?" he asked. "Milking cows," I responded. "That's right and you need to be over there with them! If your neighbors are up so should you."

I loved the summer ministry in rural Maine. I experienced neighborliness like I had never known it before. But I thought the internship was just that—a good experience, a chance to learn a lot—but then I would get on with my life. So, as the summer ended, and it was time to return to seminary, Carl cornered me in his office. "There's everything here in the world for you. What more do you want? Go look around at churches, look at all the possibilities. But don't forget these churches need you."

I did just what Carl said. I looked around and kept thinking of the people in the three churches I'd served. So, in 1975, I was installed as pastor at a service in the village church at North New Portland, Maine. Carl preached the sermon. I remember him smiling at me from the pulpit. "Scott, you have everything in the world right here. Be a good parish minister and follow your heart's delight."

I've shared Carl Geores' advice with many seminary students; I've probably said these words to Nate Phillips a few times. They're true. What Carl was saying to me was simple. Be a good pastor. Mind all the details of parish ministry. Visit the sick, preach the gospel, balance the budget. And follow your heart's delight, which I took to mean "find something in your ministry you love and pursue it."

At Mission at the Eastward, I was blessed with a great teacher in Carl Geores. Not only did he *say* "find something you love to do," he encouraged me and helped with the resources. As Nate has so ably described, Mission at the Eastward was a cooperative parish. That made all the difference in the world for me. "Never work alone," was another saying of Carl's. So, from day one in ministry, I was part of a staff of ministers. We had bi-weekly staff meetings. These were compulsory. And beyond serving a multi-church parish you were expected to support the wider ministry of MATE. You were a camp counselor, like it or not. To get paid, you had to fill out a detailed monthly report describing exactly what you had been doing. One-hundred home visits a month was the standard. I counted every human encounter. A conversation in the grocery store checkout line. That counted as a visit! The point was not to be difficult, but accountability. At staff meetings we watched one another closely. We could give expression to our hopes and dreams for the parish, and in confidence speak about our loneliness and fears. Those Sundays when only two or three gathered in the Lord's name.

The nature of the local church tends to be to look inward at its own life. The genius of the cooperative parish is to look outward. For me, my heart's delight, moved towards community organization. I cared about the rural living center giving life to an old grange building, offering home for a day care center and a library. Then there was an electronic components assembly business housed in an abandoned school, good jobs for forty people. Finally, an affordable housing neighborhood, 82 High Street, which is no longer known as "the ghetto," and offers safe and efficient homes for fifty families. "Dream big," Carl would say, and with the Mission staff and friends throughout the nine member churches, I had built-in resources to help me, encourage me, rejoice when things worked well, help pick me up when things failed. I never felt alone in the ministry at Mission at the Eastward.

I always kept Carl Geores' question before me, "what more in life do you want?" and I found more than enough to hold me in the parish in the foothills of Western Maine for thirty-five years. The churches and people of Mission at the Eastward shaped my life and gave me my life. Carl Geores taught me everything I'd need to know about parish ministry. He could be very tough and demanding but I never doubted he loved me. Thinking back over the years at MATE, the words that come to mind are "abundance" and "expansive." Western Maine can be a tough, hardscrabble place, but there was hospitality and room to grow and find your way.

I've known Nate Phillips his entire life. I had him in camp when he was a skinny, mouthy ten-year-old. I knew his grandparents before him—Milton, an evangelical preacher, and Phyllis, the kindest person in the world. Starting at Camp at the Eastward, MATE gave Nate a place to grow and try things. He was surrounded by good and able people who loved and encouraged him. College, seminary, and ordination followed. Nate accepted a call at the Red Clay Presbyterian Church in Wilmington, Delaware. But his roots in Maine were deep, and he wanted his new parish to experience all that the small churches of Mission at the Eastward had given to him. And so began a strong and vital partnership. I love the way Nate describes the current chapter of MATE, incorporating not only rural Maine churches, but including the Red Clay church and so many others, those that are caught up in the expansive, creative spirit of the place. Reading Nate's book, I wonder if he isn't the next in line of the Mission leaders—Bill Burger, Carl Geores, and myself.

Nate is a good pastor. I love his deeply moving story ("The Widow's Library") of reading Scripture from an old copy of the *Book of Common Worship* to a dying young woman. He has a pastor's heart. And, he is certainly following his "heart's delight." Nate loves the church. Nate delights in all the creative expression and experiment found in these good stories of men and women, as Larry Rasmussen puts it, "practicing creative deviance on the front line."[1] What is compelling for me in Nate's intriguing book is the way he holds together heartfelt faith with "creative deviance." I think he found this in Mission at the Eastward, which always sought to hold together the love of Jesus found in small churches with an expansive ministry reaching "the last house on the last road."

---

1. Bass, *Practicing Our Faith.*

Let's go back out to Matinicus Island. Matinicus is so remote, so far out to sea, islanders say that when they go to the mainland for supplies they're going to America. At the end of the day, fishermen come on the boat and slump down on the *Sunbeam's* cushioned benches. Their talk is about work: "shedders are coming in," "the hydraulics are broken," and "the price of lobsters is down again." I think what a rare and precious thing it is that these hardworking people have a place where they are comfortable and trust us. The *Sunbeam* feels like home.

A young woman enters the boat's salon, a stern-woman; she sits down and gets a shoulder rub from Jillian, the boat steward. The men wonder why they were not offered such treatment. They are put in their place. Samantha tells me she is close to getting her fishing license; she works with her father who is nearing retirement and wants to take over from him. She's strong, well tattooed, and very smart. She's going to college on a Sea Coast Mission scholarship; her dream is to be a pilot. Samantha says how much the Mission has meant to her and her family over the years, "I feel better just knowing the *Sunbeam* is in the harbor."

All this good work began in Bar Harbor, Maine, when two brothers— Angus and Alexander MacDonald, pastors of the Bar Harbor and Seal Harbor Congregational Churches—looked out from Cadillac Mountain over the broad expanse of ocean dotted with islands. They knew from firsthand experience there were hundreds of people living under grinding economic conditions. Surveying the picture, Alexander exclaimed to his brother, "What a parish all of this would make!" Angus replied, "Why not make it all into one?"

They set to work raising money to purchase the 26-foot sailing sloop, *Hope.* They wrote of the new ministry, *"To sail a sloop in a parish extending from Kittery Point to Quoddy Head, along the broken coast of Maine, in all kinds of weather, is not a small undertaking. To enter the coves and harbors, to call on the families on isolated islands, to visit the lightkeepers and the lifesaving stations, is a task of greater magnitude."* In 1905 it was no small undertaking to sail a small boat the entire length of the Maine coast. But what truly impresses me *is a task of greater magnitude*—to enter the lives of families living in isolated places.

Among the good things my teacher and friend Carl Geores taught me was the proverb, "without a vision the people perish." I've been privileged in forty years of ministry to work with men and women of vision, who set before me *tasks of greater magnitude.* Carl Geores taught me to have an expansive view of ministry in Western Maine and that led to some great things. Now on the coast of Downeast, Maine, I'm the heir of the Mac-Donald brothers who had a dream to sail boats to remote outer islands. Today, their vision is expressed in the *Sunbeam* providing state-of-the-art telemedicine to island communities, and old-fashioned one-on-one pastoral care to sternmen and women. For me, the ministry has always held a sense of adventure and excitement; it's been fun trying new things, to enjoy some successes, and to be discouraged at failures. I remember so well when a small electronics manufacturing plant we organized to deal with growing unemployment closed down and we laid off forty workers. People were very disappointed and afraid for their futures. But every single one of them came up to me and thanked me for at least trying to do something.

The theme of Nate Phillips' book is *practicing creative deviance on the frontline.* I believe that is what the church is called to do. The point of Nate's book is to stimulate creative and faithful thinking. It's fun and its worth a lifetime. I know.

Scott Planting
President
Maine Sea Coast Mission
Bar Harbor, Maine

Study Guide

CHAPTER 1

Read James 1:19–27

1. What changes do you think James would make if he pastored your church?
2. What are people in a rush to do? In your home? At your work? At your church? What does this say about that system?
3. Have you ever been the recipient of mission, charity, or church benevolence? What was that like?
4. What is the real, ultimate, or (even) cosmic, purpose of your church's work?
5. As you were introduced to the chapters ahead, which stood out as most intriguing?

CHAPTER 2

Read Matthew 28:16–20

1. "The Great Commission" in Matthew 28:19–20 has five verbs, "Go," "Make," "Baptize," "Teach," "Obey," and "Remember." Every church and church leader prioritizes these differently. List them in order for you and your church.
2. What priorities does your church imagine for the pastor? Can you list them?

3. Does your church imagine the pastor to be "Simple and Honorable," a "Captain," a "CEO," or a "Community Organizer"?

4. What do you think will be the primary function for future pastors? Something described in this chapter or something new?

5. Take some time to consider how pastors experience their call as a constantly moving target. How can the church be more supportive in helping them to manage "all of the above"?

CHAPTER 3

Read Isaiah 60:1–2

1. Guided by Isaiah, who writes for a community recovering from exile, consider the exilic communities in your context. How are they hearing the message, "Arise, shine, for your light has come"?

2. What does it mean for a church to be white at heart?

3. Shannon Kershner suggests that it is more faithful to include feminine language when we speak of God. How is that so?

4. Many churches reach out to dispossessed groups, how would it look different to, as Broderick puts it, "center them"?

5. Consider a person or group of people that your church can better stand and wait alongside as they seek to set their eyes on Christ.

CHAPTER 4

Read 1 Corinthians 12:12–31

1. Paul says that "God has arranged the body." What kind of body has God given to your community? How is it unique and strong?

2. Consider Matt's problematic models. He cites "geographical-historical," "community of consumers," and "church against the world." When you say "church," are you thinking of one of these models? Which one?

3. Matt says, "Thus a church building is not a problem in and of itself. But the building and its history can become an idol when they become more important than Jesus Christ." Does your church talk more about the building than it does Jesus? Does it talk about any one thing more than it does Jesus?

4. How do you understand the vocation of your particular congregation?

5. How does your community express joy?

CHAPTER 5

Read Mark 2:23–27

1. What is Jesus saying about their old rules concerning Sabbath-keeping?

2. Nanette Sawyer is dedicated to worship that networks to new community and ancient practices. How is your church networking? Where are the possibilities for more worship networking?

3. The use of technology in worship is a controversial subject. What resistance does your church have to Livestreaming, projector and screen, use of social media as worship aide, or texting to give?

4. "Find your vibrancy." Taking Oran Warder's advice, list five things that make your church vibrant.

5. How is the old, old story being told in the worship service you attend or lead?

CHAPTER 6

Read 1 Corinthians 15:58

1. Who did the labor that has been handed to your church? Who are the saints of your congregation (historical or current)? How do you honor them?

2. Instead of believing that he knew what was best for his corner of Pasadena, Cory's labor began in listening to what the community was

telling him. If you listened to your community, what would it say? Better yet, just go listen to your community. Report later.

3. Amos considers 80 percent of a worship space capacity to constitute "critical mass." What does critical mass look like for your church? What does your "mass" communicate?

4. At Union Coffee, Mike Baughman merges the ancient, traditional, and modern worlds to shape the worshiping community. Which of these worlds gets the most attention at your church? The least?

5. Which is more likely for you and your church—neglecting the new or dismissing the old?

CHAPTER 7

Read Acts 2:1–4

1. The story of Pentecost, found in Acts 2, is often called the "birthday of the church." What can the church learn about evangelism by remembering its first story? What kind of agency was left to the people? What kind of agency was left to God?

2. What is the litmus test for real ministry? Jason Chesnut doesn't often meet his congregation face-to-face—is his ministry real? Why or why not?

3. The Nave Gallery is a good example of how opened space can infuse new relationships into a community. How does your church view space? Who does it belong to? How can it be leveraged to create relationships with folks unlike your congregation?

4. "If primary motivation of your evangelism (gardening or otherwise) is saving your church, it probably isn't evangelism." So, what is the primary motivation of your evangelism?

5. As Holly is finding with the BGC, evangelism is as much about turning yourself over to what God is doing as it is anything else. How are you and your church being evangelized?

CHAPTER 8

Read Luke 9:10–17

1. What role does Jesus play in the disciple's outreach to the 5,000?

2. Discuss the difference between transactional and transformational relationships. Think of a transactional relationship in your life, then think of a transformational one. What makes them different?

3. What kind of metrics does your church use to determine how to engage in outreach?

4. "Lunch for the Soul" was a little thing that prepared the church to do a bigger thing. Is there a big thing out there for your church's outreach? What little thing might be a way to prepare for it?

5. When you and your church next celebrate the work of outreach (and you should celebrate!), who needs to be invited to the circle?

CHAPTER 9

Read John 10:1–10

1. Jesus speaks of many voices calling for his sheep. How many voices are calling for your attention? Which voice gets it most?

2. Coffee shop ministries broaden the times a church can engage with its neighborhood. What kind of schedule broadening can take place in your church?

3. Matt Overton is marrying faith and enterprise with Mow Town, he is hoping to offer this to youth as a frame for the rest of their work lives. How is faith infused into the places we work? If it isn't, how do we interpret our work through the lens of faith?

4. The Feed Truck is a mechanism for a congregation to leave the church walls to do intangible good in the community. Brainstorm one idea that mimics their work in your community.

5. If your church gets deeper into the "business of life," what do you think it will care about more than it did before?

CHAPTER 10

Read Psalm 133

1. This Scripture is a Psalm of Ascents, which means it was used to bring pilgrims together as they made their way to Jerusalem for worship. They would've been journeying from a variety of different walks of life. What tools do we have to bring different kinds of people together to cooperate in ministry?

2. Does your church concern itself more with survival than it does with mission? What are some cooperative opportunities to help rebalance the scale?

3. Where do your friends go to church? Do you ever talk with them about church? How can we shift those conversations to become less about competition and more about cooperation?

4. Does your church have any relationships that would be a natural cooperative fit, if it were not for the geographical distance? Is that distance surmountable?

5. What makes your place beautiful? How will you share it? Will it take cooperation?

MORE MINISTRY CONVERSATIONS

Youth and Children's Ministry *with Jason Brian Santos*

NP: Jason, you are the Coordinator for Youth, College, and Young Adult Ministries at the Presbyterian Mission Agency of the PC(USA) and hold a PhD in Practical Theology from Princeton Seminary. You have served as a youth minister at churches with memberships of 300 and 3,000. You are both the expert and the practitioner. Where do you see churches doing children and youth ministry well?

JS: At large?

NP: Yes, practically speaking.

JS: In the places where there is a communal theology that is lived into by a community. It is where youth groups are consistent with the corporate worship. In a lot of other church traditions, like Pentecostal and Assemblies traditions, youth groups feel like any other church worship service. Other than games, they are singing the same songs and listening to the same kind of preaching. My point is that the children and youth buy into a theology.

NP: What you're saying is that the mainline went wrong when we got away from doing the same thing at youth church as we do at big church. So, if we wanted to remedy that, would you advocate for youth ministry to look like corporate worship or for corporate worship to look like youth ministry?

JS: I would say, "Yes, they both need to look like one another."

NP: But who has to change?

JS: There is a mutual adaptation. This is why church history is essential. You have to take the larger picture of who we are and understand that change has happened. If you accept the fact that change is part of who we are, it makes it a lot easier.

NP: Fair enough. So, what kind of adaptation do we need to make in youth ministry?

JS: You know, I've spent a considerable portion of my career fighting the notion that youth ministry is just about fun and games. But here's the thing, I think youth groups could be purely about fun and games if formation was happening in the home and in the corporate body. Then, at youth group, we say, "We were first a worshiping a community, we were first brothers and sisters in Christ. We happen to be the same age, we are gathering this way, it's natural for us to fellowship together and do what we like to do, we like to play games together." But, by and large, our churches and families aren't doing that; we stopped teaching our kids and we shoved that job off to the youth minister. We farm out faith formation just like we farm out dance lessons and basketball.

NP: What you're saying is the youth ministry should be the ministry of the entire community, right?

JS: Yes. People worry that youth ministry is only for professionals, but kids will respect anyone that is authentic about where they are in their faith journey. As they see more adults invested in faith they will say, "Hey this is a lifelong journey that we share together, sometimes this goes easy, sometimes it goes hard." We've lost that communal ethos that drives us together for that journey.

NP: Getting that back is easier said than done. Asking an adult to share their faith openly with young people, even their children, is an intimidating task. How do we help people have enough courage to get started in this?

JS: We need to create a parent community. Yes, they are overworked, over-tired, and over-programmed. But instead of saying that we are teaching our parents all they need with a twenty-minute sermon, let's ask where their spiritual input is coming from. Maybe we ask them to do Sunday school with their child. We've all bought into a lie that parents and children can't do formation together, that parents need to give them their space. That used to be true when parents did formation with their kids at home, but when do you see your kids these days? Most people see their kids two hours a day. I think if parents had a better understanding of how the patterns of communities impact the formation of children, they would take more seriously the role of what it means to be in community.

NP: Are there any handholds from a specialist like yourself? Do you have a few things a church might do to try to create this kind of community ethos?

JS: Let's do things in an intergenerational way. I'm not saying we get rid of "ages and stages." I'm saying we've shifted to doing only "ages and stages." Now kids only go to children's church and youth group and they think that is what their entire spiritualization is about.

NP: But if you were headed to a church to be its pastor or children's ministry leader, what would you do?

JS: At my last church, I created one giant Sunday school class. The youngest was three years old and the oldest was ninety-two.

NP: So, how did that go?

JS: It was phenomenal. The kids saw that faith isn't learned just among their peers. It's something that people of all ages are doing. It got teenagers to hear the stories and share in experiences with folks in the church they may not have known. We acted out stories, one week we did an art project. We sat around a big canvas, read passages, and shared questions while they painted something. The implicit curriculum was that we could learn together.

NP: You are talking about a significant shift, but part of me thinks you just have to stick with this for a little bit. Over time, the people that stay will see the impact that can happen. That's part of the problem, we want our churches to be overrun with kids tomorrow, and there is no quick fix.

Ministry with Millennials *with Hardy Kim*

NP: Hardy, you serve at one of the flagship churches in the PC(USA) and spend a considerable portion of your time working with millennials, how is your heart rate?

HK: I will admit, it is an uphill battle all the time in terms of building community and program. I put community first, intentionally, because I'm not sure millennials care that much about program. But building any sort of structure, to build commitment and ownership, is difficult because the majority of the members of the group don't want to take official long-term commitment of the group. When I say long-term, I mean a year or two.

NP: And that's frustrating for church people. Especially for Presbyterians who say, "Three years is a standard commitment." I feel like the old man sitting here, waving my cane, saying, "You entitled children. You need to pay your dues." But I don't know if we can afford to do that. I get the feeling they can kind of shrug at us and say, "Everyone else wants our attention. We'll take it somewhere else."

HK: Yes, but they all are looking for relationships. I feel like this is something that expresses the best of our tradition, that we can hold young adults as they struggle through some very difficult times, but that is also a source of great joy for those who get involved. I think that a key for my role in doing this is a little paradoxical—I am very much a Gen Xer who isn't shy about questioning their commitments or their way of life, but I also can see myself in their struggles. When it comes to the latter part, it is more my experiences of frustration, alienation, and failure that allow me to relate to them, not my successes or wisdom about how to overcome these things.

NP: Beyond your pastoral voice in their lives, both challenging and caring, what else is clicking in your work with millennials?

HK: I think we are tending to the question of acceptance and community and having people you can count on. I think for the young adults that are coming, there is a fragility to their life. Even the ones that have a good job, and seem like they have everything going on, there is a fragility to their lives.

NP: That's the first time I've heard someone say that. In general, when people talk about millennials, it is like they are the cool kids at high school.

Everyone wants to be like them; everyone wants to dress like them. But you're saying, "No, no, no, you have start at the beginning—at the base level of their lives, which is just as fragile as anyone else's."

HK: Think of how they've grown up. Since Junior High they have been protecting an image and competing for that image. Yes, we the church tend to see them as this sparkly shiny thing and think that if we could only get them attracted to us, we'd be all set; but there is a spiritual need there.

NP: OK, so let's talk about community. If you are a church that wants to cultivate something like what you're doing with millennials, does it have to be just young adults or can it be mixed?

HK: That's a good question. I think there's a part of it that has to be just young adults, and that's not because millennials don't like people who are older than them. It is because it can be so tricky for them to let their guard down and get real about who they are. Dating is so different from previous generations. They live in a world that is okay with a "hookup culture," drinking, and drug use. If you put them together with people from other generations they think, "I can't really be that honest about my life."

NP: OK, but I'm trying to be a little bit of a problem solver here. What if you don't have a big church with enough young adults for a freestanding program? Give me one option that might be helpful for churches trying to create a space where young adults can share their faith.

HK: I could see churches combining with a couple of other churches to get a group of young adults for a retreat. Offer them good food, good drink, good conversations, a chance to turn off mobile technology, and get to know one another really well. One of the best retreats we had was on technology and relationships. Another really good one was about faith and sexuality. They were asking, "Why isn't the church talking with us about this stuff?" They went into their free time talking about these issues because they were so engaged.

NP: It sounds like we have to create some transitional program between youth group and "church as we know it." Then there's a part of me that's like, "church as we know it" isn't the end goal here.

HK: I think that is where we are at. I think the nature of community is completely different. What does that mean about the sustainability of the church? I have no idea. If churches want to keep on doing the things they've done the past, then forget millennials because energy courting them is energy wasted. If people of faith are willing to venture out to do community differently, that's a different story.

NP: Which is sort of the point of this book. Thanks for that.

Diversity in the Church *with John Molina-Moore*

NP: John, not only are you biracial, you grew up in a very diverse church. You have served two very different, but mostly white congregations. You come at the question of diversity in the church with real life experience. So, what is your insight? Why is the mainline church so segregated?

JMM: For me there are two reasons. First, we have to look at our social circles. If we want our churches to be diverse, the rest of our circles need to be diverse.

NP: What is the second reason?

JMM: Most mainline church services are made for white people. It comes down to systemically changing a lot of stuff we do. You can't want to be diverse and do things in a very one-cultured way.

NP: That reminds me of a time on World Communion Sunday, we had a visitor from South Africa visiting the church. I thought it would be awesome if they would read Scripture in Xhosa, their own language, alongside the English. I asked our lay reader if he would read the English. He was very upset that I would do that. He asked, "Why would I do that? Nobody is going to understand the Xhosa." I thought, "First of all, the people that are from South Africa will." But there is this resistance to welcoming in any kind of foreign thing because, "Who is going to understand it?"

JMM: It's a tricky game to play. Do we just bring in something foreign because it's the right thing to do, even if nobody from that culture is there? Or do we wait until people show up and then start doing it because they are there? I think you do it because it offers a more expansive way to know and understand God. Who cares if it's all white people sitting in there?

NP: That's the point. If we do this, we get to see God better. So, outside of worship, how does a church know if they are getting at the question of diversity?

JMM: I know that a church is conscious about it if I can be myself there. I don't have to do my double talk or code switching like I have to at my kid's PTA meeting and at work. I actually have a place where I can fully be myself.

NP: You grew up in a church like that.

JMM: Yes, that church was multi-cultural.

NP: You felt like you could be yourself there?

JMM: Yes. We sang gospel songs. We sang songs in Korean. There was an actual attempt because it was authentic to us. Take my current church. Last communion Sunday, I asked a Cameroonian man to do a traditional prayer that would be used at a communion service in Cameroon. I should've known, but it ended up being a seven-minute-long prayer. I was totally expecting to hear complaints but received only awesome feedback. I still hear, "That was so great to have him do that."

NP: But if we start saying we are going to be intentionally diverse about the way we do worship, the way we run youth ministry, the way we do everything, and then it's still only white people coming, we are going to be asking, "What's the point?"

JMM: Sure. But I don't know anyone that's doing that and still has only white people coming. You can't do a bunch of programming that satellites what you're doing and not infuse it with the actual culture of your church.

NP: OK, so what does that look like?

JMM: I think the future multi-cultural church is going to be made up of people that aren't currently going to church. It is going to be people that don't have that in the bloodline, not folks that have been handed church down to them from generations.

NP: What you're talking about is doing evangelism with people unlike yourself. Somebody moves next door, number one, are we going to be friends with them because they have a different color skin than we do? Maybe. But then, you just assume that they won't be interested in your worshiping community because they have a different color skin. That is what we do, we make assumptions.

JMM: But if you actually get to know them . . .

NP: The central point of all of this is how we form relationships with people and have evangelism be born out of that. Not that you are just inviting people to church, but that your relationship with God is evident in your approach to your friendship. You let those friendships blossom no matter what color skin they have and that might make it so our churches look different.

JMM: Yes, but then when folks show up it is our responsibility as leaders to make sure there is a tone of welcome no matter what they look like. I can remember one of my first services preaching at a white church, we sang one of my favorite gospel songs, "Every Time I feel Spirit," and one of the members came to me after worship and said, "That wasn't very Presbyterian." We can't continue to be like that and expect our churches to be diverse.

A Multi-Faith World *with Edwin Estevez*

NP: Edwin, you are doing some really interesting work in engaging faith traditions outside of your own. What is your first take on the topic, "A Multi-Faith World"?

EE: First, let me give you my context. Growing up, I encountered all sorts of faiths. My mom cleaned homes, often for Jewish families, so we were invited to Bar Mitzvahs and Bat Mitzvahs. Then, within my family, we had a variety of Christian traditions represented. We have Pentecostals, Quakers, Methodists, and Lutherans. I grew up with devout Catholics who believe that anyone that is not Catholic is not Christian.

NP: Sounds pretty exclusive.

EE: Yes, they'd often evangelize us. They'd send me the rosary. Then, on the other hand, I had these Pentecostals in my family telling me that Catholics were going to hell. I had these two sides of my family.

NP: Both really exclusive to their own traditions. How did that go for you?

EE: It made me very interested in the God question. I've been drawn to Jewish friends, Mormons, Jehovah's Witnesses, and asked a lot of questions. I grew up with this debate. I've had to really think through my Christian faith. This was especially true when my sister married, Faicel, a Muslim man.

NP: Tell me that story.

EE: Well, she went to Spain and took a ferryboat ride to Morocco. There she met her tour guide, Faicel, who would then become her husband.

NP: How did that go with your family?

EE: When they were dating it was cool. When they decided to get married, we kind of freaked out. But he's a very devout Muslim and he's a really good guy, so we came around pretty quickly.

NP: How was that for him? How does your family's Christianity intersect with his faith?

EE: Yes, good question. He was having his own crisis. He went to a Holy Man and said, "I'm in love with a Christian woman, what do I do?" The man kept telling him to keep exploring it. Over time, he finally said, "Your job is to be the best Muslim you can be, and help her become the best Christian she can be." That was his wisdom.

NP: Powerful stuff.

EE: Yes, when he shared that we all felt at ease. We knew that he was not trying to convert her, but support her in his walk of faith. Now he will come to church with her. He came to my ordination service, for instance. She will prepare the food for Ramadan. It is a lot of negotiation.

The most beautiful part of it, though, is that my family is asking, "Who is Jesus?" in a new way. We grew up in a Christian household and took it for granted.

NP: Wow. So his presence in your family has insisted that each of you re-examine your own faith in a way that hadn't been required of you before.

EE: Yes, our faith has been stirred up again.

NP: The church often finds itself paralyzed by the task of navigating a multi-faith world, but you were pushed into it. Can you give the church some advice as it tries to become better at this?

EE: Right, the fact is that a lot of churches don't talk about it, so it's the elephant in the room. Or, when they do talk about it, it is in a disrespectful way. But the church can no longer afford to avoid this conversation. By the time I have children, it will be guaranteed that they will be going to school with many children of other faiths. As we connect and find the good in other faiths, we can see this as the gift of an opportunity to rethink faith. It is like the early Christians who had an experience to be a minority. It will lead us to go deep into our faith.

NP: Do you think that churches can be part of the kind of relational connection you have with your brother in law?

EE: Yes, in some ways. I think it can start with hospitality. I think about how Jesus focused on hospitality. Also, in Islam there is a high priority on hospitality. Finding that connection point could be really valuable. I could see churches intentionally opening their doors to say, "You know what, you guys are welcome to use this as a space for prayers." This will invite people to feel more than tolerated, but embraced. Then hopefully the Spirit moves and friendships are created because of it.

NP: That seems like a real stretch.

EE: I know. I think churches are afraid of it. They think that, suddenly, they would lose members. However, a church that is vibrant and has a healthy sense of self wouldn't feel threatened, but see it as an opportunity to grow our faiths.